I'm So *Over it.*

When You've Had Enough of Failed
Relationships, Self-Sabotaging Habits, and
Irritating Trends in Dating

Kierra C. Jones

HOUSE CAPACITY PUBLISHING
DETROIT

I'm So Over It
Copyright © 2017 by Kierra C. Jones
Published by House Capacity Publishing
Detroit, MI
www.housecapacity.com

For booking and purchasing information please visit
www.kierracjones.com.

ISBN: 0692894381
ISBN-13: 978-0692894385

To the One whose love and pursuit has never ceased to amaze me. The One who has never given up on me even when I gave up on Him. The One in whom I live, breathe, and have my being: Jesus Christ.

To my big girl, Kasey: I hope that I make you proud, baby girl. I would give the world to you if only you asked for it.

To my mother and father, I weep at the amount of support you've given me throughout this entire process. You believe in me when no one else does. You motivate me to keep going and keep shining.

Acknowledgements

I want to thank Christopher "Doc" Reid for your support and counsel! You helped me scratch up some things that I thought were buried! You held me accountable to change, and you challenged me to be greater each and every day. I am indebted to you.

Special thanks to Yatara Reid for being a true fairy god-mother! I am so grateful for your support!

Aleka Thrash at ACT Photography: thank you for the AMAZING photos! You made me look wonderful, per usual! I also thank you for your friendship, counsel, tough love, and support. You and me, us never part!

To Paige Wright at Radiant Enrichments: you truly made me shine from the inside out. You beat me into a coma, girl. The make-up was flawless!

I also want to thank all of the family and friends who have lent their ears, prayers, support, sponsorship, blessings, counsel, and assistance.

Join Our Facebook Group!

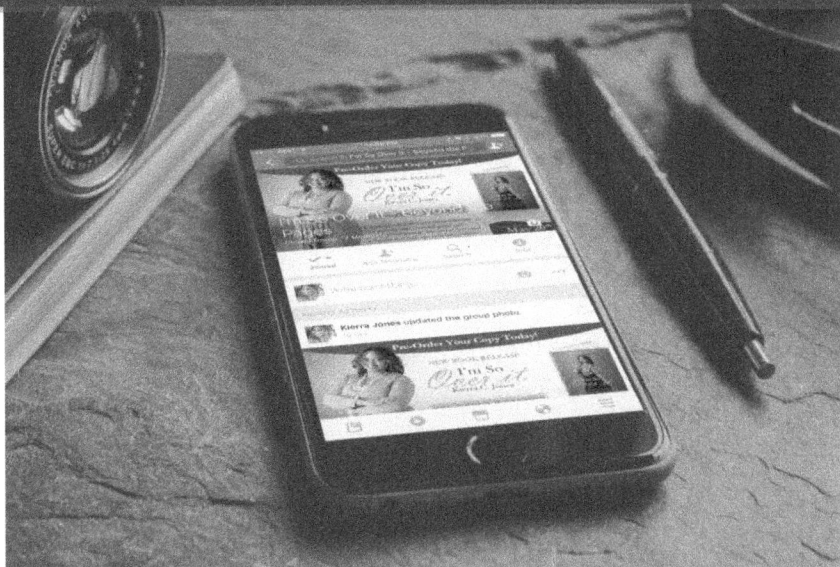

I'm So Over It – Beyond the Pages

This Facebook group is designed to support single women in their journey experiencing love, relationships, motherhood, and more. We hope to provide a platform where women may speak openly about their struggles and well as their triumphs; we want to offer encouragement and enlightenment to every woman who connects with us!

Anticipate experiencing:

- Live interactive videos from author Kierra C. Jones
- Group meet-up events
- Book club discussion-based questions
- Tips and tools to be a savvy single

Scan to join!

Contents

I'm So Over...

To the Nunnery

I think that my friends are tired of me threatening to become a nun. As a matter of fact, I don't think that they even believe me anymore—okay, they've never believed me, but I've been pretty consistent with this thing. Nunnery has been my constant threat to my friends (and God) in response to what seems like an unrealistically terrible love life. Nuns take a life-long vow of celibacy. They don't lie awake at night wondering why Rakeem won't call them back. Sister Holy-Lady doesn't wonder why Tevin is liking all of Nyesha's pictures but isn't responding to her texts. A good ol' nun isn't stalking the page of the girl who posted hearts on her crush's Instagram picture. No. Nuns are not posting subliminal statuses and memes directed towards an ignorant man about how "every man will regret mistreating a good woman". Nuns just devote their entire lives to pleasing God. To feeding the poor. To visiting the sick. To putting on fancy musicals with high school kids…?

I thought that this kind of life was better than trying to focus on being in love with a man. When I *really* became fed up with my love life, I actually looked up the qualifications for being a nun! I found out that I was ineligible anyway. Can't have any dependent children under the age of eighteen. Darn. I just shrugged after the Lord told me how utterly ridiculous and dramatic I was being for even looking it up.

Surely, it was not my desire to become a nun, it was my lack of faith. Honestly, the whole dating, falling in love, and getting married thing had seemed to be a cruelly elusive possibility for me. What's crazy about it is that I am actually content being single. I'd rather not be single forever, granted, but it seemed like every time I opened myself up to the potential of dating someone, it backfired. I almost wanted to go through life with a t-shirt that says "#LeaveMeAlone". I'm not one who feels like I am only complete and whole when I'm with someone else, but I do feel like if I was going to abandon my awesomely single life and let someone into that space, the relationship should at least have the nerve to work out!

I've read all of the books on dating and relationships. Some of them two or three times. Actually, if I read another one, I'll probably throw up. I know not to have sex before marriage, I know that I need to have great self-esteem, I know that I need to make sure that I only choose a guy who's "after God's own heart." I know that I should "wait" and that I should let God "write my love story". Although I was well read, I felt like I was applying all of these principles and not getting any further in my love life than if I hadn't read them at all.

So, I decided to have a conversation with God about me being "over it". I had to be open and transparent with Him so that I could really get the answers that I needed. In my honesty, I came up with some things that irritated me to no end about my own dating and relationships fiasco. After much reflection, I came to the realization that the problem was not so much with love as it was with—me. I had some terrible habits and ways of thinking that really caused me to sabotage my own emotional well-being. I was even more annoyed that I had no one else to blame but myself. So, with every bout of toxic thinking and destructive habits, there had to be some resolution. For God's sake, there had to be some way to break the cycle!

There may be others out there who have also felt that having a successful relationship was a myth. Maybe you still feel that way. I invite you to look at every frustration though a different lens: what can you learn? How can you grow and develop from the crappy experiences that you've had in the past? How might your thinking need to be altered so that you don't continue the same cycle? Before you submit your application to the convent and forsake love, please follow my journey to healing. I am still growing and learning, but God, I'm not in the same place. So get some hot tea and get comfortable while we discuss the hot mess that was my love life!

chapter 1

I'm So Over

"I Love You"

So, I'm flying down the freeway, tears streaming down my face, pushing about 90. With each minute that I was on the road, the rain seemed to be pouring down harder and harder. I was out here feeling like a Temptation thinking about how the "raindrops would hide my teardrops". My soul had been shaken this day because I had discovered the foulest form of betrayal. The man who had declared his love for me, and who I had reluctantly declared mine for, decided to be in a relationship with someone else.

I think the biggest stabbing in the back surrounding this discovery was that I had just spoken so highly of him to one of my closest friends. I bragged about some of the poetic things he had told me—how he loved the scent of my hair and could tell whenever I had so much as changed my shampoo. I told her all about how he would hold me—how he had looked deeply into my eyes and told me that he loved me. I even shared his intentions to start a family with me "someday".

We went through a few cycles of "break-up to make-up," and while I was going on and on about how great he was, it was during one of those break-ups. I was actually thinking that it was about time for us to patch things up. Imagine my saltiness when I went to his Facebook page and saw that he was in a relationship with someone else—a "someone" who I had already suspected that he was still involved with. The embarrassment was too much to bear, though I tried to act like I wasn't really phased by my discovery. But he *loved* me though. How could you love someone and so easily decide to be with someone else?

— · — · — · — ··

I finally slowed the car down and controlled my rage a little to talk to God. I screamed out, "Why does this keep happening to me?! Why did you let him do this to me?! Do I deserve this?!"

And as calmly as He could answer, he said, "Kierra, *you* did this. How could you expect it to work when I am not the foundation? How could you expect him to truly love you when he doesn't truly love me? You strayed from the path that I set for you, and so you reaped from the seeds that you've sown."

I was irritated with that answer. While God was completely correct, my heart was still in pieces and I needed some way to relieve my pain—or I at least needed to find some type of temporary fix. I didn't feel like praying or worshipping God. I didn't feel like rendering up a "shondobohotah" in the spirit either.

Waiting to Exhale

So I burned his stuff. I know, I know. It wasn't a very "saved" way of dealing with my emotions. It shocked me, but I tapped into my inner Bernadine, exhaled," and lit some ish on fire. Now this "stuff" that I burned was really only a single book that he had given to me to read, but it was symbolic of his very presence in my life. I fell more and more for him with each page that I read. It was the way that we

> "I lit some ish on fire."

became connected; it was the key to everything that had transpired between us since he had placed it in my hands. So it had to go.

That stupid book was almost indestructible because it took me so long to actually get it to catch flame! If we were still cool, I definitely would ask him who printed it! I poured bleach on it, Listerine, oil—I guess you could say that I'm not the expert at vindictive strike-backs. Eventually, I was more upset that the book wasn't burning than I was at his actual betrayal! But once it began to burn, baby, it was euphoric. Watching those flames mutilate and melt those pages was almost the closure that I needed. I felt it appropriate to light a cigarette to commemorate this grand occasion, but I don't smoke—besides, there was enough smoke in my lungs from the fire in my kitchen sink! While I was physically burning a book, I felt that I was symbolically burning love. I felt that I burned every desire to have it or for it to have me. That night I was content with either possibility.

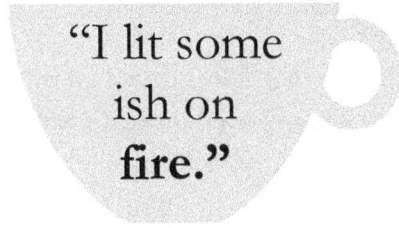

I Love the Way You Lie

I think that every man that I'd been in a relationship with in my entire life has told me that he loved me. Sometimes it came at the end of a two a.m. phone call when we both knew that we had to get up and get to work in the morning. Sometimes it came out of the mouth of some stupid teenage boy who just thought I was pretty enough to "do it" to. There were times when it came after a night of heavy panting and sinning, or after a heart-to-heart conversation about where I saw us "going". Nonetheless, they all said it—and they all lied.

Now, I won't play the blame game completely because I've told guys that I loved them without really knowing what I was saying. I interpreted the fast beating of my heart and the giddiness that I felt around said guy as love. My "I love you" came as a result of seeing everything about that person and deciding that I adored it all. It was the result of being infatuated with his physical appearance, his smile, the words that he spoke, and other things that had no bearing on what it truly means to love someone.

More Than a Feeling

In my "studies" of love, I determined one absolute truth: love extends well beyond what you feel at the moment. After those butterflies in your stomach go away, after he stops being so sweet and considerate, after he has gone a few weeks without a haircut, after the cute little dates have gone on pause, do you still love him?

I've come to the conclusion that love is more a decision than it is a feeling. It is the decision to say, "I'm going to treat you with respect and honor even when I don't think you deserve such treatment." Or maybe, "I'm going to do what it takes to support your dreams and goals even if I am inconvenienced every now and then." My pastors once told me that no matter how upset they may have been with each other, they agreed to always kiss each other good night. I can't imagine what a kiss between two people who were butting heads all day looks like! Ha! But they were deciding to show affection even though they didn't feel like it. Some very wise married men and women told me that on the days that you don't like your spouse, allow your love to conquer all. It's deciding to maintain the foundation of love to carry you through even if you're not having feelings of warm and fuzziness.

Love Has a Standard

One of the hardest things that I had to do was letting go of someone who told me he loved me but did not exhibit the qualities that love is always supposed to stand on. I was in shambles trying to figure out if I should let him go or stay in the relationship to work things out. I even talked about the situation with a private women's support group that I was a part of on Facebook to get advice from some of the ladies. One of the most profound responses came from a woman who I'd never met in person, but you couldn't tell me that she wasn't one of my bff's. She told me to do something very simple, and once I completed this task, it told me everything I needed to know so that I could do what I needed to do.

"Look up the biblical definition of love found in 1 Corinthians 13. Everywhere that you see the word 'love' or a pronoun representing love, I want you to replace that word with your guy's name. If those statements are true then you might want to see if you two can get past what you're going through. If most of those are not true, then I think you already know what you need to do."

And so I completed her task, and once I was done, tears streamed from my eyes. I had to leave him because he was not love. Never mind the fact that if I had put my own name in those blanks, I probably would have passed. The fact of the

"The **strength** of my own love was **not enough** to influence his love."

9

The Love Test

1. _____ is patient and kind.
2. _____ does not envy or boast.
3. _____ is not arrogant or rude.
4. _____ does not insist on (his) own way.
5. _____ is not irritable or resentful.
6. _____ does not rejoice at wrongdoing, but rejoices with the truth.
7. _____ bears (or covers) all things.
8. _____ believes all things.
9. _____ hopes all things.
10. _____ endures (or is willing to sacrifice) all things.

matter was that I was with someone who was choosing not to be these things for me, and the strength of my own love was not enough to influence his love. He did not live up to love's standard.

It's crazy how we sometimes think that because we love someone we have to accept any old thing and call it love. That simply isn't true! I had to learn that even though God loves us beyond what we will ever understand, He still has a standard for how we are to love Him! He tells us in the Bible that if we love Him we are supposed to keep His commandments, that we are to love no one above Him, and that we must not worship anything else beside Him! If the creator of the universe has things that He requires from someone who says that he/she loves Him, then why don't we?

Lust: Love's Alter Ego

We can't truthfully have a discussion about love without bringing up love's alter-ego, lust. I remember when everybody was up in arms about Beyonce telling everyone that she had an alter-ego named "Sasha Fierce". On the surface, Beyonce and "Sasha" looked exactly the same, but they differed entirely in their character. In my assessment, "Beyonce" was mild-mannered and more reserved, whereas "Sasha" was more bold and daring. So it is with love and lust: they might look the same, but they behave entirely differently. One basic difference between lust and love is this: love seeks to give, lust seeks to get. If you're not careful, you might mistake one for the other!

Amnon ~~Loves~~ Lusts Tamar

In the Bible, there is a story about a man who claimed to be so absolutely over-the-hills in love with a woman, that he claimed he felt sicker each day that he could not have her.

> *"O son of the king, why are you so haggard morning after morning? Will you not tell me? Amnon said to him, "I love Tamar, my brother Absalom's sister."*
> (II Samuel 13:4)

We're going to ignore the fact that technically Tamar is Amnon's sister, too. I said ignore it. Okay, fine it creeped me out. Instead, let's talk about what Amnon did to show this "love" for Tamar. He pretended to be sick and asked his father, David, if Tamar could come by his house and cook for him. David granted his request; Tamar was his sister, after all.

When Tamar came to Amnon's chambers, he requested that she stay and cook the food in front of him and that she feed it to him afterwards. Tamar obliged. Amnon quickly ordered all of his servants out of the room so that he was left alone with Tamar. When she came close to him in order to feed him, Amnon grabbed her and asked her to have sex with him!

Of course, Tamar being a virgin, denied his request and begged him not to defile her. In her plea she said, "Where could I carry my shame?" She even suggested that he go to their father, David, and seek her hand in marriage. Amnon knew that if he raped Tamar she would not be able to marry any other man and that it was against the law for him to have sex with her if he was not her husband. The fact that she had to give him a reason to not violate her was already an issue! Amnon didn't care anything about what Tamar had to say; He raped her anyway!

Let's pause and remember how much Amnon "loved" Tamar and was so lovesick over her at the beginning. It's crazy that after he was done, his "love" immediately turned to hate and he kicked her out! Amnon didn't love Tamar at all, he lusted her! He was motivated to get something from her, not to give her something from himself. Love does not insist on its own way, and it covers: if he loved Tamar, he would have put his own desires aside and done what was best for her. He knew what sleeping with Tamar would cost her, and he defiled her anyway.

— · — · — · — · · —

Which brings me back to my book-burning ceremony. I was upset with myself for being so upset about his new relationship! I was so hurt because I felt like it was too easy to give up on what we were establishing. Looking back on my relationship (or lack thereof) with this guy, he never exhibited anything close to love anyway! Forget the fact that "I love you" sounded so beautiful coming from his gorgeous lips, his actions never checked out. I was accepting the alter-ego of love!

One of the reasons why we were up in the air and off-and-on all the time is because we both were selfish when it came to our own desires. We didn't always operate with the best intentions for the other. I wanted to believe that he loved me, but he was not willing to take on love's persona, and to a certain extent, neither was I.

While we're claiming to love people and accepting them telling us the same, let's really look to the word of God as the standard! Let's make our actions align with our words and require the same from the people who have declared their love for us. I don't plan to burn anything else in the future, but I do plan to exhibit the love I wish to receive!

There is no fear in love. But perfect love drives out fear, because fear has to do with punishment. The one who fears is not made perfect in love. We love because he first loved us.
(1 John 4:18-19)

Be Done with It...

1. Are you in or have you ever been in a relationship that was centered around lust? How do you know?

2. Complete "The Love Test" on page 10 placing your own name in the blanks. Do you measure up to what the Word of God says that love should be? In what areas do you need to improve?

chapter 2

I'm So Over

Breaking Up

I've had this experience more times than I care to count: breaking up with someone but still wanting to hold on for dear life. Even though the relationship was clearly over, I found some way to continue being connected to my exes. When one relationship was over, I decided that we could be colleagues and continue our "professional relationship," but that was a pitiful excuse. The real reason why I wanted to stay connected to them is because I didn't want to deal with the pain associated with losing them. Breaking up sucks. You spend all of this time getting to know someone, developing feelings for someone, investing in someone, trusting someone—only to find that this person really isn't right for you. Here comes the "speech" that one of you has to give about not being "ready" for a relationship or some other excuse. Then come the days, weeks, and months that you have to spend trying to heal from a broken heart and learning how to move on from that relationship. It is not an instant process, and the agony seems significantly greater than what it actually is. I'm tired of spending time doing social media "drive-by's" on the guy who I was no longer dating—only to be upset by what I find. I am so over this process!

The "Break-Up" Process

In my own experiences with breaking up, I would be so upset with myself for still have feelings for the guy or for still being in a terrible funk after the break-up. I would want to slap myself and say, "Move past it! Ugh!" What I had to realize is that I needed to feel what I felt and that I could not rush past the process. Just like the stages of grief that people go through during death, there are stages of grief that we usually experience when going through a break-up. These feelings don't always happen in order, and there may be one or two that we don't experience at all. I think that at least knowing that these feelings could exist is a great way to be self-aware so that you know how to appropriately manage all of your emotions.

Denial

I won't say that I've felt denial every time I've broken up with someone, but it does surface from time to time. You want to believe that you two will make up or that you just need some time apart. The reality is that the relationship is over, and probably has been for some time, but you don't want to handle the flood of emotions that come with truly accepting the relationship's demise. I was in such denial that one of my relationships was over that I was still coming around hanging out with him and his family! That begot all types of awkwardness! Somehow, I convinced myself that we could "still be friends." I was still doing things for him that I had done in our relationship, but then I had the nerve to be upset with him because I felt that he was taking advantage of me! How?!

It was clear that it was over, but I didn't want to accept it. And because of my habit of putting my head in the sand, I couldn't really move on, appropriately deal with my feelings, and heal.

> "It was **clear** that it was over, but I didn't want to **accept** it."

Anger

Ooh, baby, have I experienced this. Probably every time a relationship ended. My anger was shooting out in all directions, too: anger at myself, anger at the guy, anger at God. I would be vexed at myself because I felt that I should have been able to see through his charm and gorgeous exterior to recognize that he was a terrible person to be with. I'd replay situations in my head and scold myself for ignoring the red flags that were waving like crazy.

I'd be angry at a guy because I would feel like he really missed out on a good woman. I'd run through all of the things that I did for him and all of the positive qualities that I possessed—in my head I would call him every name except a child of God. It was a slap in my face for a guy to be in the presence of such awesomeness and then decide to leave it behind. How dare they?! In the height of my anger I would contemplate doing some vindictive things—and man, my mind was coming up with some tripped out plans to get even! There are some names that I hear and still think, "If I ever catch him in the streets…". Ha! Pray for me.

I feel like I was a little too bold to be angry with God because

17

I don't want to know what it is like for Him to be angry with me! Yet and still, I held a grudge. I'd think, "Lord, you knew that he would mistreat me or that I wasn't the right fit for him! Why didn't you give me the heads up?!" The reality is that He had been giving me several warnings and signs, but I didn't want to listen! Even though he gave me signs, I would be angry that He didn't just send a good man my way so that I could be done with all of the heartache and foolishness.

> "You don't attract who you want, you attract who you are."

His response? You don't attract what you want, you attract what you are. What's that sudden saltiness I'm tasting? Clearly there was some work that I needed to do in order to undo the cycle! What was inside of me that sent out a message that I was a beacon for ill-suited men?

Bargaining

My version of bargaining looked a little different depending on the relationship, but for the most part it was a similar conversation with myself. A lot of times I would blame myself for lacking in some area and then think that if I fixed that "thing", I could patch things up with my ex. If the ex and I never got back together, I still thought that fixing my perceived issue would qualify me for being with an even better man in the future.

One time, I held on to that thought that if I had been a little more giving or a little more accommodating, maybe the relationship would have fared better. So, in my mind, I resolved to either show him that I could be those things or be extra giving and accommodating with the next man. Huge mistake! Then sometimes insecurities would try to take over and I would think, "He must not think that I'm that attractive anymore. Let me make sure that I slay the next time he sees me so that he would re-think the breakup. If I'm looking my absolute best, he wouldn't be able to resist me!"

Be extremely careful when you are in this phase of the break-up cycle! With bargaining also comes the temptation to bargain with your standards, especially if you believe that you are the entire cause of the break-up. Of course, break-ups are rarely just one party's fault exclusively, but many times, grief strikes and you find yourself missing him and reminiscing about the good times. Grief could cloud your judgement and make you conveniently forget about some of issues that may have been good reason to end the relationship. For example: if one of the reasons why you decided to end the relationship is because you felt that he didn't view you as a priority, being in the bargaining stage of grief could easily cause you to compromise the expectation to be a priority in his life. You may be tempted to make excuses for him and his ability to make time for you. Sometimes you can bargain yourself right back into the arms of the same issues.

Depression

And then there's depression. If you've never had some kind of feelings of depression, consider yourself blessed. In many ways, breaking up with someone is like experiencing a death, especially if the relationship had any type of depth. This is the stage that I try to fast forward through so that I don't have to feel like my heart has been blended into somebody's morning smoothie. There's the crying. The eating. The re-reading of the text messages. The social media stalking (or the traditional stalking). The feeling that life cannot possibly go on apart from him. I've literally felt like there would be no end to my agony.

Let me interject a little bit here with a discussion about soul-ties. It's my best guess that if you've been in such a depressive state as the one I described above, then you've most likely had a soul-tie with an individual. What's a soul-tie? I think it's best described as a knitting together of one's mind, will, and emotions with another individual. This means that whoever you are connected to in this manner has influence over the way you think, the things that you do, and the way that you feel. To analyze this definition even further, the way that you think and feel already impact your actions, so when someone else influences all three, imagine how vulnerable you could be to that person!

So how does this "knitting" happen? I think that it can happen a couple of different ways, but the most powerful way to establish a soul-tie is through sex. The Bible tells us that when two individuals give their bodies to each other, they become "one flesh". God purposely designed sex in such a way that we would experience a deep connection with the other person because the purpose of sex is to consummate a marriage. It's like God already created a wonderful thing (marriage) and then added sex as a bonding agent to make it even better. Sex was designed to be ministry between husband and wife.

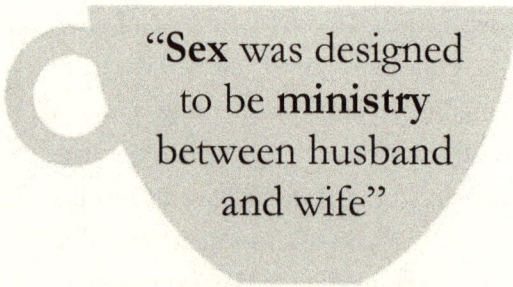

> "**Sex** was designed to be **ministry** between husband and wife"

The soul-tie that forms in the marriage bed was meant to be strengthened so that the mind, will, and emotions of both husband and wife could continue to be influenced by each other. This type of bond or influence was never intended to be broken.

Now, insert you and me—or some of our friends—who've

20

experienced sex outside of the will of God. We still experience this type of bonding or knitting together, but we also experience the breaking of the bond, which God never intended for us. If sex means that I become one in body with the person that I have sex with, then I am supposed to experience excruciating pain when that person is no longer a part of my life! That's like walking around all my life with two arms and legs and then someone decides to push me down and rip one arm and one leg from my body! What pain! I view the pain of breaking a soul-tie as a safety mechanism that God installed in sex so that if married people ever tried to break away from each other, the pain would be too unbearable for them to do so.

The problem is that many of us single people are forming these soul-ties with our "boo's," "bae's," or whatever we're calling them at the time. We don't have the same grace to endure the responsibility or risk that comes along with being one with somebody. God is the one who blesses the covenant between man and wife, but that same covenant grace and favor is not on us when have sex outside of his will!

Acceptance

It is my earnest prayer that anyone who has experienced a break-up eventually makes it to the acceptance stage. This is when all of your feelings stabilize and you're able to really examine the relationship with a more balanced point of view. You are able to make a self-assessment of where you went wrong in the relationship and even forgive your ex for the things that he may have done wrong as well. Not saying that just because you forgive him you two can be together again—it's just that now you're not allowing hurt and anger to rule you. You may be able to use this experience as an opportunity for growth, and you may be able to

Kierra C. Jones

The Break-Up Cycle

*adapted from the Kubler-Ross Five Stages of Grief model (1967)

• **Denial** — Having a hard time accepting that the relationship is over. Persons in this stage may think that the relationship is still salvageable despite all of the signs that suggest that it isn't.

• **Anger** — Being upset with oneself or the individual responsible for your heartbreak. This stage may include irrational acts of vengeance or a demonization of the ex.

• **Bargaining** — Attempting to compromise your standards and preferences in order to revive the relationship, or attempting to make adjustments to suit the other party's prefererences, even if those preferences are unreasonable.

• **Depression** – Extreme feelings of sorrow and pain while enduring a break-up. Usually intensified by a soul-tie with your ex.

• **Acceptance** – Being able to assess the former relationship from a place of wholeness and wisdom. Posessing the ability to forgive your ex and yourself for any transgressions. Bonus: experiencing a newfound swag and confidence.

readjust your behavior in preparation for a healthy relationship. You adjust, you heal, you move forward. This is an awesome place.

Better yet, when you're in the acceptance stage, you're not really interested in having a romantic relationship with your ex again. But be warned: when you've truly accepted that the relationship is over, it is likely that your ex will try to spring up and pull you right back into the trap! It's almost like they get an alarm that says, "Mayday! Mayday! Bruh, she's over you!" Egos will never allow that, so sometimes people come back sniffing around not because they even want you, but because they can't stand you not wanting them. The nerve! Also, during the acceptance stage, you start to regain your swag. Your eyes aren't puffy anymore from consistent crying. You're no longer wearing that "I'm one second away from popping off on everybody" t-shirt. Ha! You're not coming off as bruised and desperate, and you look and feel revitalized. You're werking it.

Now, I will emphasize that the main objective of healing from broken relationships is not for the sake of attracting another man, but I will tell you this: after I allowed myself that time to heal and be restored, I had to beat the brothas away with a stick! I must have had an extra umph in my walk, or there must have been an extra sweetness in my aura 'cause they were on your girl, okay? But even in this awesome place of acceptance, we still have to be wise about who we allow access to our hearts! Just because you can attract them doesn't mean that they are suitable for you! You still must be discerning and be intentional about protecting your heart. Don't get so caught up in your new found dopeness that you put yourself into a position to experience yet another heartbreak!

A Word to the Bound

I just want to encourage you and tell you that God is able to restore whatever was lost as a result of being connected to a toxic or ungodly relationship. In Nahum 1:13, God tells Ninevah that the yokes of their bondage would be broken from them. That means that you can also be set free from whatever bondage that you are experiencing from the result of being connected to your exes—whether that connection is physical, emotional, or otherwise. Those individuals will not be able to have a hold on you. It means that if you surrender those feelings and emotions to God, liberty is available. God is able to remove the impression that any man has on you so that they no longer have any bearing on your destiny.

He heals the brokenhearted and binds up their wounds.
(Psalm 147:3)

Be Done with It...

1. Chapter two focuses on the "Break-Up Cycle": have you ever found yourself experiencing one of the stages (other than acceptance) longer than the others? What factors do you think aided in remaining in that stage for so long?

2. Do you have a soul-tie with an ex? If so, what could be something practical that you could do in order to sever that tie?

chapter 3

I'm So Over

Fixing the Damaged

I was having a conversation with one of my good friends, who happens to be highly qualified at reading people and making all types of accurate assessments. He told me something so true but so shocking about myself: I had a horrible tendency to attract men who needed some type of emotional "fixing". I mean, the track record was scary: the one scarred from divorce, the one who felt abandoned by his family, the one who had been hurt and used countless times by women he loved, the one who had been disowned by his drug-addicted mother (who was also born addicted to heroin)—the list continued to grow.

My good friend went a little further and gave me a visual I will never forget:

Every time you feel like rushing in to save a man from his emotional baggage, I want you to picture yourself in a fireman's uniform. Baggy, oversized, and just ill-fitted. I wish I could show you what this looks like so that you can see just how ridiculous you look.

Into the Fire

There was one who I definitely suited up for: and I was willing to rush in and endure the flames as long as I could! I thought I'd met my perfect match. When I met this man, I was immediately drawn to him because I could sense his love and passion for God. He seemed to have a genuine concern for bringing people into the saving knowledge of Jesus Christ, and I was hooked! It also helped that he was fine! My interest in him grew exponentially. He was like no one I'd ever met before.

The first time we talked on the phone, our conversation lasted for six hours. Yes, I said six hours. I was a grown woman on the phone giggling and smiling with someone all night long. I felt like I was sixteen again. What I loved about our conversation was that it was one hundred percent pure. We shared our beliefs, how we came to be Christians, silly habits that we had, how we grew up—everything. It was such a relief to meet someone who was living a lifestyle that I was striving to live. Our connection was instant. He was a breath of fresh air.

As we talked more and spent more time with each other, we began to share more intimate details about our lives. I admit, I was a bit thrown by some of the things that he revealed, but I was still smitten by him. I appreciated the level of transparency and honesty that he displayed. I was glad that he felt comfortable enough to be that vulnerable with me. Even as I shared things about myself, he didn't judge me. He was understanding and supportive. We even committed to praying with each other and studying the Bible together. He was the one leading all of this. This had to be a win.

What was also keenly different about my interaction with him versus anyone else I'd been interested in was the fact that I was one hundred percent on board with his vision. I could see myself helping him expand his ideas, and I even had a few ideas of my own. I actively worked on things that would help him with his goals, and I enjoyed every moment of it. My skills and gifts seemed to be an added bonus to the groundwork he had already laid. His project also became mine, and it was euphoric. We worked extremely well as a team, and I wanted to be by his side as he expanded to new levels. By this time, I was already picking wedding colors and thinking of a timeline for our wedding events!

As we continued to see each other and work together, we began to clash. I noticed that the relationship changed from this perfect God-centered blessing to something entirely toxic. We would frequently get into arguments, and they would end with us not speaking to each other for days. I was a wreck. He seemed to get angry

"The relationship changed from this perfect **God-centered** blessing to something entirely **toxic.**"

at the simplest things, and I didn't know what to say or do to divert that anger. I was often confused about why he was so angry. We spent less time together, and he displayed a lot of jealous and possessive behavior. He began to talk to me like I was beneath him, and I began to feel undervalued. I felt like I was walking on eggshells after a while. I felt like he no longer cared about my feelings or the relationship. I was sick and sad consistently, and it didn't seem like we could get on the same page to make things work. I tried to share my feelings and concerns in hopes that we could salvage what we had, but I was met with more anger, more condescension, and more accusations.

Imagine my despair. I thought I got it right this time. I just knew that God presented me with someone who was great for me, but then I felt like the enemy had set me up and that I had blindly bitten the bait. I lamented about this situation to anyone who would hear me. I was completely hopeless. I attempted to understand why our relationship had taken such a nosedive, and I was desperate to find a way to fix it. I did not want to let him go.

That was exactly what God told me to do. Fall back and let him go. I cried and cried and accused God of being cruel and unfair. I was so sure that He had given me the okay to get close to this man, only for me to end up hurt in the end. But then God explained things a little more. He said, "Have you ever tried to hug a cactus?" Then I envisioned what it must be like to do that. I imagine that the harder you squeeze, the more those sharp edges will hurt. I noticed that the more I tried to love and understand and embrace, the more I began to hurt. I remembered the words that my pastor had repeated numerous times, "Hurting people hurt people."

God also revealed to me that I wasn't the balm that this man needed, He was. Although he had been saved and delivered, was anointed, and in ministry, there was still some residue from his past that needed to be dealt with. As much of a "fixer" I was, I couldn't fix that. I had to give him up entirely, and trust that he was best kept in God's hands.

This was sort of like the woman with the issue of blood: other physicians attempted to heal her, but she received healing only when she came to Jesus (Luke 8:43-48). I even had to abandon the hope that we would eventually be together, because if I didn't, I would be tempted to hug the cactus again.

Cactus-Huggers, Anonymous

For the life of me, I couldn't figure out why I was attracted to such dysfunction: I myself didn't have any of this type of baggage. I considered my heart quite healthy, actually. Then once I dug a little deeper into my tendency to play "shero," it began to be crystal clear why I, and perhaps, other women, felt that it was our god-given duty to rescue men from their brokenness.

Caught Up in Fantasy and Potential

My mother probably should have named me Hope because when it came to relationships, I had a crippling habit of seeing a man or relationship, skipping past the reality of the relationship, and getting to the good part where we'd be smiling and skipping alongside of the beach. But what about the part where he's talking to me like he's crazy because that's how his mom talked to him? Fast forward, that won't last long. Or the part where he says he doesn't even believe in marriage anymore and that it's all just a false sense of hope? He'll come along because I believe in enough love for the both of us. And please skip past the part where he says that he can't connect to a woman emotionally because his heart had been broken beyond repair. I seriously thought that the relationship's potential could undo any negativity that was present in our current very real relationship. I was very wrong.

The conversation often went like this for me: "Sure, he's not giving me what I need emotionally, and he's not reciprocating the love that I am pouring out on him, but eventually he'll be so full on my love that he'll have no choice but to pour it back into me. This is a minor discomfort when I think about what I will gain as a result of loving him correctly!"

Sound a siren, please! There is no guarantee that this man will wake up one day, have a "come to Jesus" moment and think, "Dang. I'm so full on her love that it's only right for me to start loving her the same way." There is a strong possibility that this man can drain you of all the love that you have to offer him and never return it. Why? Because he is emotionally damaged, hun. He cannot love from a place of strength and wholeness because he is weak and broken. Hear me: if he is not in a position where he's willing to exchange his heart with yours and love fully and purely, then he won't. It won't matter how richly you love him because he will be receiving your love from a place of damage and hurt.

It's like this: when people go to a hospital, they do so because they expect to be treated for some type of ailment, sickness, disease, etc. They don't expect the doctor to come in after the treatment and say, "So now that I've healed you, we can talk about my needs. I've had this terrible headache...".

You'd look at him like he was crazy. I'd probably actually say, "I'm the patient, and you're the doctor. How could you expect me to know the first thing about treating you?" As a matter of fact, once patients are healed, they don't keep sticking around the hospital, they go home and resume their lives! They don't come back to the hospital until it's time to be treated again!

The same with this hurting, broken man. He may only view you as the solution to his heart problem, but more than likely it will be a one-sided love ordeal. If you're playing love doctor, you have to anticipate that once he's "healed" he will then walk away from your "situationship" entirely.

I'm So Over It

So I've learned to abandon the fantasy of his potential to love me someday, and if you're loving on a guy who is damaged to the degree that you are the only one giving in the relationship, then you might need to abandon him, too. You have to ask yourself if he never changes could I be happy with this type of relationship forever? If the answer is no, then you need to move on.

"He may only view you as the **solution** to his heart problem..."

The reality is that the emotionally damaged guy is not in a place to love fully and unconditionally because he still needs to figure out what that actually requires from him and whether or not he's actually willing to make that sacrifice. This requires a type of healing that you, even with your huge heart, cannot love him through.

Feeling Guilty about Abandoning Him

If you're like me, then you've been a sucker for fine men and sob stories. Lord, help me. You feel like the guy who you have been dating was vulnerable enough to share his deepest hurt and pain, so you'd be a jerk if you abandoned him after being exposed to the source of all of his grief. You almost feel a special connection with him because you felt like he trusted you enough to let you in on such a sensitive aspect of his heart. It's in that moment that you give him the power to manipulate you based on those feelings.

Even though being connected to him might make you feel more negative than positive, you don't want to leave because you feel like he needs you right now. Never mind the fact that the relationship is all about him and his needs, you feel like leaving him right now would make you just like all of the other people in his life who failed or hurt him, and you just can't have him think of you in that way. You love him. You only want to be there for him and give him everything that his heart longs for.

So you stay and realize that your expectations of him become lower and lower because any qualms you may have always go back to "Well, he told you that he had a hard time trusting women. You already know he's healing. His heart is in a vulnerable place. If I ask too much of him, I may push him away."

Listen here. You are not responsible for anyone's healing or emotional baggage. It's not your job to restore his hope in the female race. It's not your job to carry the weight of the burden he carries from his past. It's also not beneficial for you to pacify him and never challenge him to be better. He has to make the decision to initiate his healing process. That is a decision that could be influenced by him meeting you, or maybe it won't be. The point is that he needs to decide for himself that he is ready to be healed whether you stick around or if you don't.

This reminds me of an incident in the Bible when Jesus came across a man who had been disabled for thirty-eight years. The man had been lying by a special pool waiting for the angels to bless it so that he could get in and be healed. The problem was that every time this "blessing" of the pool occurred, he had no one there to help him, so he remained in his disabled state. Jesus asked him a powerful question, "Do you want to be whole?" That's when the man went on and on about the obstacles preventing him from achieving wholeness. I can imagine Jesus rolling his eyes after hearing the excuses—so much that he told the man, "Get up, take up your bed, and walk (John 5:8)." The man did as Jesus said, and he was immediately healed.

There are two points that I'd like to make from this particular

Bible story. The first is that before Jesus even healed the man, Jesus asked him if even wanted to be healed. Jesus could have just walked by, saw that the man was clearly paralyzed, healed him, and went on his merry way. I believe that it was very important for Jesus to ask this question because he had to make sure that he wasn't working against the man's own will. That is the first step to anyone's healing: first deciding that they no longer want the pain. Some people are okay with holding on to their pain. Some have learned to become one with it and never decide to heal and experience wholeness. The emotionally damaged guy that you may have fallen for must make the decision to be whole on his own, otherwise you may find yourself and your love working against his will to remain damaged. The second point that

"You may find yourself and your love **working against his will** to remain damaged."

I'd like to make is that the paralyzed man thought that he needed someone else's help in order to be healed. He waited thirty-eight years for someone to help him get into that pool. THIRTY EIGHT YEARS. Sound familiar? Some men will make you think that they can't "get right" unless they have your help, or sometimes we think that he can't be healed unless our help is instituted. The reality is that if he has a personal relationship with Jesus Christ, he has what he needs to be whole! Now, I'm not saying that we don't need help in this journey and that we don't sometimes need people to hold us accountable, pray with us, or even cry with us. What I am saying is that if you are attempting to take the place of the miracle-working power of Jesus Christ, or if he is casting down his cares upon you like you're Jesus, you're sure to lose. Jesus can take on such heavy burdens, we can't.

If he truly wants to be healed, he has to be able and willing to do so even in your absence. If your decision to leave causes him to forsake you and rue the day he ever met you, he isn't at an emotionally mature place to be able to be healed on his own accord. You don't want to be the captain of his destiny and the person responsible for his happiness. That baggage isn't yours to unpack for him.

Ego/Insecurity

I've got to admit: I have an ego. I think we all do to some degree, but I've learned how my ego could get the best of me, especially when it came to entertaining men who claimed to be emotionally damaged. I've literally had men tell me verbatim, "You should probably go and find someone who can give you what you need, because it isn't me." I should have done exactly what they told me to do, but no, I did the exact opposite. Now the guys who told me this could have totally been gaming me, but in my mind, I had to expose them to the wonder that is Kierra. I expected that because of their exposure they'd never be able to let me get away.

I just knew that because I was such a good woman, I could inspire any man to do away with the baggage from his past. because of how great I am. Now, it's perfectly fine to be a confident woman. No one wants to be with a woman who is insecure or one who has low self-esteem (actually, there are plenty of men who prefer women like this, but that's another book). The problem comes when that confident woman starts trying to prove that she is the good woman that the man needs in his life. Her natural confidence turns into a performance for his approval.

Before she knows it, her confidence becomes rooted in insecurity because she begins to start looking for his affirmation. She wants him to be impressed. She wants him to be smitten by her awesomeness. She doesn't realize that because he is damaged, he is not able to respond appropriately to anything that she does to "prove" herself. Because he doesn't respond to her with the love she wants in return, she thinks it's because of her own shortcomings and not because of his.

This is not okay! I strongly believe that any man I decide to give my heart to should make me feel more secure about my love for him, not cause me to question whether or not he thinks I am enough. The truth is that you are enough for someone. You're just exhausting all of that glory and splendor on someone who is looking at you through a hazy lens.

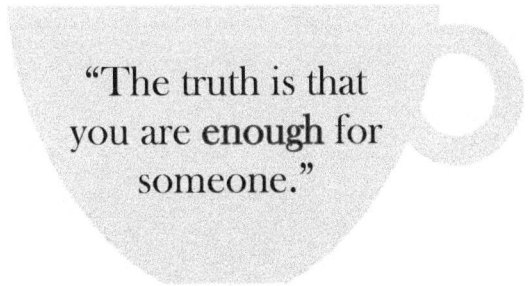

> "The truth is that you are **enough** for someone."

When I was in college, I took a class that was all about how the eye functions (the most boring class in life, but I needed it to fulfill one of my gen-ed requirements). My professor gave us an assignment to partner with someone, smear Vaseline on a pair of reading glasses, wear them, attempt to identify people, and function for 30 minutes without removing the glasses. Of course we failed. I couldn't recognize anyone who came into my eyesight even if they were right in front of me. My partner would ask me things like, "What type of facial expression am I making?" and I would be completely clueless.

Think of the emotionally damaged guy as someone who is wearing a set of Vaseline-smeared glasses. It doesn't matter how obviously great you are, he won't be able to recognize it fully. The way that he views you is skewed due to the fact that he only sees you through the hazy lens of pain and damage.

I'll ask you flat out: are you in a toxic relationship? Who are you holding on to? I know that women love hard, but sometimes we can love someone best by carrying them to God and walking away.

Come to me, all who labor and are heavy laden, and I will give you rest. Take my yoke upon you, and learn from me, for I am gentle and lowly in heart, and you will find rest for your souls. For my yoke is easy, and my burden is light.
(Matthew 11:28-30)

Be Done with It...

1.   Are you in a relationship with someone who is emotionally damaged? What may be some indicators that this person is not in a healthy emotional/mental place to participate in a relationship with you?

2.   Do you find yourself trying to "fix" or rescue a person who is experiencing some kind of emotional damage? If so, why do you have the desire to do so?

chapter 4

I'm So Over

Dating While Damaged

onsider this: it's one thing to try to play nurse and patch up someone else's bruises, but it's another thing when you attempt to connect with someone without dealing with your own damage! I know first-hand because I was still dealing with the pain of a break-up, and I brought all of that stuff and dumped it onto somebody else.

Truthfully, I knew I wasn't in a good place to really connect myself to someone else. I even pledged to go at least six months without dating at all, per the instructions of a book I was reading at the time. I started to feel like I was okay and that I had moved on, but then someone else came along vying for my attention. At the time, he was saying all of the right things. He looked kind of saved, and seemed to be pretty nice. I thought that it would be harmless going out with him—the whole "take time to heal between relationships" thing was just an exaggeration, right?

The first conversation that I had with the new guy was—okay. There were no sparks or little angels singing while we conversed. Those white doves must have been on vacation, because none of them were flying over us in loving approval. Then I thought, "Kierra, you're clearly basing this conversation on the six hour marathon you had with the guy you were dating before. At least see how well you connect with this one on the first date."

Then the first date came, and still, no fireworks. I admit, he was interesting. He shared some things that definitely had my eyes wide the entire time—but my eyes were wide mostly because he shared a lot of shocking things that he probably should until like date three or four to share! I thought that our energy was friendly at best, but I didn't really see anything special coming out of our meeting.

He had some projects going on that seemed interesting. He even wanted me to be a part of them, but I wasn't very enthusiastic about his vision. I didn't go into "helpmate" mode when he explained all that he wanted to accomplish. I actually had the tools, knowledge, and skills to help him move his vision forward, but I didn't have the energy or desire to even get my hands dirty. I didn't feel like who I was aligned with who he was, and so I didn't really feel a connection with him.

Hol' Up!

He, however, had a completely different analysis of "us". I immediately became all sorts of "bae," "sweetheart," "my love," and the like. He told me repeatedly how wonderful he thought I was, and how great we would be together. This guy didn't hold back any punches. He was planning our life together, and I found myself screaming in my head, "Hol' up!" He was falling in love with me in record time. I felt like things were going uber fast. Have you ever seen someone walking with a toddler? Those babies almost look like they're being dragged because of how fast their little legs are moving to keep up with their parent. I felt that I was being dragged along, and I was extremely uncomfortable with the pace of this pseudo relationship.

Welp, the guy that I was dating previously reached out to me as I had figured (and hoped) he would. When we talked, the entire chest that I had stuffed with my emotions exploded. It seemed like everything I had felt for him was magnified ten times over, even the negative emotions. I thought that we had enough time away from each other to clear our heads and work things out. Nope. Not at all. More arguing, more anger, more of me trying to be understanding and accommodating.

I was mentally and emotionally right back where I started after we "broke up" the first time. I was in a vulnerable and broken place. Shortly after this phone call, I immediately explained to the new guy that I wasn't in a place to really date and get to know anyone. I really had to be honest with him and myself. I told him that I needed to heal in some areas and that I didn't mean to waste his time. He wouldn't hear it. Instead, he tried to

> "He tried to **convince me** that I wasn't **as damaged** as I thought I was ..."

convince me that I wasn't as damaged as I thought I was and that my ex was just trying to ruin my future. The more I tried to explain, the more he tried to convince me otherwise.

Savage

I was convinced that this love-stricken guy and his wide nose wasn't going anywhere, and so I did something horrible. I used him. Even though I knew there would be no future and no "us", I enjoyed him treating me like I was the most beautiful woman that he'd ever set his eyes on. I enjoyed him being caring and catering. I reveled in all of the special attention he was giving me, but I had no desire to reciprocate any of it. I did not want him. I became completely selfish and animalistic: I entertained him for as long as he could benefit me. I was completely detached from his emotions, desires, and expectations. Once everything was all done away with, I didn't recognize myself. I was a savage.

God's conviction swooped in on me like you wouldn't believe. He reminded me again that "hurting people hurt people." I was obviously still dealing with and processing my own hurt, and instead of giving it to God, I hurt someone else. I received a text message from the new guy explaining that he wanted to marry me and that he'd do whatever it took so that I could be with him— and then I felt like crap.

I sat down with him and explained that I did not have the same desires that he had and that I was wrong for allowing the relationship to go on as it had. I told him that I was very much still healing from my past relationship and that I had used him as medicine to treat all of my open wounds. I told him that I was very much still connected to the guy I dated previously and that I wasn't willing to give that much of my emotions to anyone else at that time. He was crushed. I respected his feelings, and we decided not to see or speak to each other anymore. I felt like a complete jerk.

If I learned nothing else, I learned that people need to date from a place of wholeness. I was eating my own words, because I had already experienced being with someone who was not whole! I already knew what it felt like to want to love someone who was emotionally unavailable! I knew what it felt like to have never received the love I gave. My, had the tables turned! We can't use other people or relationships to patch up our wounds. We just create a cycle of brokeness if we don't take the time to really allow God to heal our hearts. I created another hurting person, and who's to say that he won't hurt someone else because of me? God is the only one who can set us free from the bondage of the past; we can't use people to do what only God can do.

> "Who's to say that he won't hurt **somone else** because of me?"

Also, even though I'm strongly convinced that a marriage wasn't in our future (mainly because he wanted to marry me after only knowing me for about two weeks), what if I met someone who was a good fit for me? I probably wouldn't have been able to make a true assessment of that man or any other man because I was emotionally damaged and emotionally unavailable. I didn't want to give my heart to anyone else. I was wrong for entertaining someone knowing fully well that I wasn't in a healthy place emotionally or spiritually.

Now, someone might come to my defense and say, "It's his own fault, you told him that you weren't ready!" I would agree to a certain extent. As women, we make this mistake all the time: we sometimes try to convince a man to choose us by doing all types of things to prove our worth. I've been there before, so I understand why he wouldn't accept me telling him of my emotional unavailability. We have to remember the quote by Maya Angelou made famous by Madea, "When someone shows you who they are, believe them." I'm sure my actions showed him that I wasn't invested in a future with him, but he chose not to believe it. I'm definitely not justifying treating him the way that I did, but hopefully in his own time he was able to reflect on our relationship, learn from his mistake, and forgive me.

New Juice, Dirty Cup

In the mist of the hot mess I created, God gave me a crazy revelation related to dating while damaged. I was getting ready to fix a cup of juice for my daughter, who was a demanding impatient two-year-old at the time. When I went to retrieve her sippy cup, I noticed that it was still dirty from the last time she had juice. Of course, I wasn't going to just put new juice into the dirty container: I put it in some dish water to let it soak a little. In the meantime, little Miss toddler Kasey was livid. She was screaming and crying like I had completely disregarded her desire for juice!

But even in the midst of her tantrum, I took my time and made sure that her cup was completely clean before I allowed her to have the juice. And then going a step further, I didn't want her to have the same juice that she had grown accustomed to—I decided to blend up a mixture of kale, strawberries, bananas, grapes, and pineapples because it would be a much healthier option for her.

Many times, we desire for God to bless us with a partner or mate, but we're still carrying around the filth and residue from past relationships. How can we pour new juice into a dirty cup, or how can we expect to have a healthy relationship with someone else if we haven't taken the time to heal? If we haven't allowed God to make us whole? And, we have to be careful who we connect ourselves with because he also might need to undergo the same healing process.

Not only do we need to heal from the damage of past relationships, we need to go a step further and renew our minds! I've heard that the definition of insanity is to do the same thing over and over again and expect different results. When I decided to give my daughter the fruit and vegetable smoothie instead her usual juice, it was because I had grown in my knowledge of nutrition. We need to seek God and be one with Him so that He can give us a fresh perspective on the type of people that we should allow in our lives! We need to ask Him to reveal the traits, habits and character of people who will sow positive seeds in our lives.

It is okay to be alone for a while. It's okay to take time to work on yourself, take care of yourself, do a little bit of soul searching, and truly heal. Not being in a relationship won't kill you, otherwise I would have died many times over. But I believe that it's worth it to take the time to become your best self—at least so that your worst self doesn't harm anyone else.

He restores my soul. He leads me in paths of righteousness for his name's sake.
(Psalm 23:3)

Be Done with It...

1. Why is it best to take time to heal before you open yourself romantically to another person?

2. Have you ever rejected someone because you were emotionally damaged? What effect did your rejection have on the other person?

chapter 5

I'm So Over

Wack Pursuit

There were plenty of times in my dating life when I was able to shake off the residue of a past relationship and open myself up to meeting someone new. But then, after dipping my foot back into the dating "pool," I noticed something that irritated my entire soul: men I encountered didn't really know how to pursue a woman!

Such a man was actually someone who I had been acquainted with for quite some time. We had crossed paths, we knew a lot of the same people, and we both supported each other in our various social media endeavors. I was actually surprised to know that he was interested in me because we never actually had a face to face conversation before. We also didn't spend much time hanging around each other because we lived on complete opposite sides of the state.

But this man was gorgeous! Heaven, be my witness! I mean, smooth chocolate skin, cheekbones for days, a dazzling white smile, piercing eyes, an immaculate physique—he was art! When he reached out to me and expressed that he wanted to get to know me, I was excited about the possibilities. I gave God an air fist bump because I just knew that He had presented me with a fine man who was everything that I wanted and more. We decided to start texting (irritating, but I digress) and eventually that led up to a phone conversation. I quickly discovered that this wasn't the type of dating "situation" that I wanted to take part in.

Who's Pursuing Whom?

Part of what soured my taste for the Black "David" was the feeling that this man was used to women fawning over him. It felt like he was never required to do much to win the affections of a woman. It was clear that he was used to doing the bare minimum in order to secure a place in a woman's life. I noticed that a lot of our conversations would be more about his physical appearance than most of the things that mattered to me: his level of spirituality, his intellect, and his creativity. I felt like I was being treated like a fan and that it was an honor for me to have his attention. He wanted me to be the one doing all of the texting and calling, and he didn't make a conscious effort to show me that I was someone who he valued and wanted to get to know. He made me feel like I was one of many options. I wasn't here for any of that, so I made sure that he had one less option to choose from.

"It was clear that he was used to doing the **bare minimum…**"

Every upstanding man in my life has told me that men have a hunting nature. I've never heard a man say, "My wife just kind of

I'm So Over It

fell into my lap, and we went from there." No! These men told me that men live for the thrill of the pursuit. They told me that a man will go above and beyond to secure the woman who he wants. Besides, I've seen it! I mean, look at King David! Michal's father told him that Michal's dowry was 100 Philistine foreskins. David literally had to probably kill 100 men and cut the skin off of their penises to marry the woman he wanted. The average man would have probably told Michal's father to "have a blessed day," and he would have ridden on to the next man's daughter. Not David! He came back with those foreskins in a bag and took his bride!

Shoot Your Shot!

And speaking of knowing how to pursue a woman, I've noticed that other men who I've encountered have the mentality that the pursuit is in the hands of the woman. Case and point: I've known a certain guy for years now, and I will say that he's grown up to be quite the hottie. I know that he's been thinking the same about me (insert overconfident emoji here). Our interactions have been somewhat awkward, but we still managed to show some type of minimal interest in each other.

One day we were texting (there's that again), and I happened to mention to him that I was a "distant admirer". About a year later, he brought up my "distant admiring," and said that it really made him feel special. The problem? He said that I didn't do anything about it. What?! I had to go metaphorical on him. I told him that I passed him the ball and that he didn't "shoot his shot." His clever response was that he only shoots high percentage shots—I'm guessing he meant that he only pursues women he feels confident that he can secure. So, I responded that perhaps he needs to tap into his inner Steph Curry—which was my insinuation that he needed to step out of his comfort zone and go for the shots (or women) who are not so easy to score with. They are worth it in the long run.

Reiterating my overarching theme: I was over it. In lieu of this conversation and all of the basketball metaphors we were throwing at each other, I came to the realization that some men pursue women much like the way that some players play basketball! We can gauge a man's pursuit style and use his actions to figure out his intentions! I would love to let you all think that I came up with this on my own, but I had the chance to vent to my good friend, Chris Hunter, and we spent time analyzing a few men.

The "AND 1" Sensation

When I was in middle school, I went through a tomboy phase and had a thing about wearing men's gym shoes. One time, my mother caved, and she let me get a pair of Iverson's. I was so geeked because my shoes came with a copy of an "AND 1 Mixtape." My brother and I went crazy watching all of the tricks that the players performed. Shoot, we even took a basketball outside to try to master some tricks of our own.

If you've ever watched any "AND 1 Mixtape," you'll notice that the emphasis is never on the players' ability to score. In fact, there are times when a player could have shot ten baskets in the amount of time that it took to demonstrate one trick. The videos highlight the showiest performances in street basketball, and the more extravagant a player is at showing off, the more admirers go crazy. My favorite player was "Hot Sauce"—mainly because he was really cute—but also because he was a genius at handling the ball. He made his opponent look like a clown after he had unleashed all of his skills.

There are some men who approach love and relationships much like an "AND 1" player. Some men who pursue women don't do so because they want to secure a promising future with a woman; they do so simply for the fun of it. Such a man could get really fancy with what he says, he can take you out, and make you think that you are the queen of his universe—but he has no intentions on making a commitment. He's entered the dating scene with the expectation of experiencing the most enjoyment he can at the expense of the women he entertains. He's showboating, and some of us just eat it all up. He has no problem with "shooting his shot", but he'll do it knowing full well that he's going to waste your time. He's the Prince of Petty: he might not respond to you for days, or make up an excuse about how he's been working so much so he hasn't had time to spend with you, etc. He might be juggling a few women at a time. Women who allow these types of men to maintain space in their lives look like a fool for entertaining the games. Please don't get "Hot-sauced". There are plenty suitable men out here who don't come with the intention to waste your time.

> "He has no intentions on making a **commitment**"

Even in the "AND 1" videos, you can often see the opponents' frustration waiting for the player to stop with all of the games and actually attempt to score. I know firsthand how frustrating it can be trying to wait for a man to get himself together so that you two can move forward and build a great relationship. Sadly, I never bode well with this strategy; eventually you have to get tired of the trickery and games and decide to leave him showboating on the court.

The Master Assister

This is the guy who doesn't need to be dating anyone right now. Seriously. For his sake and for the sake of the women he may encounter. The Master Assister might have a lot of confusion exploding in different areas of his life, but he still wants to "see what happens" or "be friends (with benefits)." No! Ugh! In basketball, players are applauded for their ability to pass the ball to another player who is in a better position to score points. The other team's defense might put a little too much pressure on the player for him to shoot a successful shot, so he passes.

The Master Assister is the guy who needs to pass. He is not in a position to pursue you seriously. The "defenders" putting pressure on him might be his own insecurities, financial issues, emotional baggage, spiritual emptiness, or even your own expectations of him. He's being blocked with so much of his baggage that he might even recognize that he might not be the best person for you. Depending on how selfish he is, he might continue to entertain you because he wants to benefit from having you in his life. It may be that you make him feel comfortable and that you don't require for him to arise to any real standards.

The Master Assister is content with being with you until you or the woman that he truly wants requires more from him. A lot times women complain about the men in their lives not making a commitment or not putting forth a lot of effort in the relationship, and it's because he isn't compelled to deal with the issues that may jeopardize his place in your life. He's not that inspired to change and grow.

The Paint-Pointer

When people think of players who can dominate the paint, they think about the greats like Shaquille O'Neal, Carmelo Anthony, and Ben Wallace. However, some men have a dating style like these paint players: they only go after opportunities that are the most confidently obtained—like that ol' buddy of mine. This is quite different from the Master Assister because the paint-pointer is not anticipating something better coming along nor is he lacking the ability to shoot. He stays close by and seldom steps out of his comfort zone when approaching women.

I'm So Over It

Let's study one of the aforementioned NBA players, Shaquille O'Neal. Homie can dunk, lay-up, and do all types of awesome things near the basket. He's had years to perfect his ability to perform in the paint, but no one looks to him to shoot the 3-pointer. In fact, his average three-point percentage is only 4.5% (Basketball-Reference.com). He's not going to voluntarily shoot it either. As it relates to dating: the point player only pursues a certain type of woman. This is not to say that his "type" is not good, it's just that he's not that open-minded in his selections with women. He may approach these women with the same methods, lines, and actions because his formula works for the type of woman that he is comfortable with pursuing. When he meets a woman who is a little different from his normal interests,

"When he notices that his **formula** doesn't work, he **retreats** in his pursuit."

and when notices that his formula doesn't work, he retreats in his pursuit. He's thinking like Shaq: "I only have a 4.5% chance of being successful with this attempt, so I'm not going to even try."

The Half-Court Courter

I'll admit: despite my knowledge of basketball lingo and rules, I'm no die-hard sports fan. If someone is watching sports and I happen to be in the room, I might take notice. During one championship game, I actually read a book! What I could not ignore, however, was one particular game when Steph Curry shot a basket from half court and made it! My social media pages were lit! The memes were crazy: someone created one that showed Steph on the outside of earth's atmosphere making a shot into a basket on earth. Clever, right?

I made up in my mind that night that Steph was the man.

The "Player" Line-up

- **The "AND 1" Sensation** — He's entered the dating scene with the expectation of experiencing the most enjoyment he can at the expense of the women he entertains. He has no problem with "shooting his shot", but he'll do it knowing full well that he's going to waste your time.
- **The Master Assister** — the guy who needs to pass. He is not in a position to pursue you seriously. He may be dealing with financial issues, emotional baggage, spiritual emptiness, or even your own expectations of him.
- **The Paint-Pointer** — He's not that open-minded in his selections with women. He may approach these women with the same methods, lines, and actions because his formula works for the type of woman that he is comfortable with pursuing.
- **The Half-Court Courter** — They are not intimidated by women who are educated, successful, or by women who possess any other positive attributes. They understand how valuable it is to have a high caliber woman, and they do not allow insecurity or ego to keep them from such a woman.

Once I started to really learn more about him as a player, I realized that the epic half-court shot that had caught my attention was not the only one he had made! I began watching video after video of Steph making shots from impossible distances! Even his practice videos showed him making endless attempts to shoot the ball from as far away as he possibly could.

Then it hit me: there are some men out there who take the Steph Curry approach to pursuing a woman. Just as Curry has shown that he is not afraid to take a seemingly impossible shot, there are men who are not intimidated by women who may seem "out of their league." They are not intimidated by women who are educated, successful, or by women who possess any other positive attributes. They understand how valuable it is to have a high caliber woman, and they do not allow insecurity or ego to keep them from such a woman.

I think that every smart man should want to marry a woman who already has her own party going on. He should want to marry a woman who has multiple strengths and talents because all of those wonderful things enhance him in a marriage. Proverbs 31:23 tells us that the husband of the virtuous woman is celebrated among the city elders. The Half Court-Courter understands the favor and grace that is available to him simply because he married a wonderful woman!

The Gist

I am worth pursuing. You are worth pursuing. I am worth someone making me a priority and worth someone willing to spend his time, energy, and resources on me. I've learned that if ever I'm placed in a position where I feel like I'm auditioning for a spot in someone's life, then it would be past time for me to make my exit. I am a prize, and I don't need to put on a grand production of my qualities to secure any man's affections.

Kierra C. Jones

---

*I can never escape from your Spirit! I can never get away
from your presence! If I go up to heaven, you are there; if I
go down to the grave, you are there.*
(Psalm 139:7-8, Message)

Be Done with It...

1. Do you believe that it is necessary for a man to actively pursue a woman? How could one determine the interest of a man who does not put forth the effort to pursue?

2. Which of the men in the "Player" Line-up have you been connected with? Was their pursuit desired?

3. What steps could you take to make sure that you are not the one pursuing a man while dating?

chapter 6

I'm So Over

Being "Found"

*N*ow, in lieu of this whole concept of pursuit: I'm not a woman who believes that all of the effort of the dating relationship should be on the man. I think that women should also show interest and be very clear about our intentions. I don't think it's wrong with a man knowing that a woman likes him. I don't think there's anything wrong with a woman making herself reasonably available to a man who she is interested in. The problem for me is when the woman is putting forth more effort than the man to progress the relationship.

According to Proverbs 18.22, "He that findeth a wife findeth a good thing and obtains favor from the Lord." I get that. A man is supposed to find his wife, and a wife should seek to be found. Cool. The issue that I have with this whole concept of "being found" is that a lot of us good ol' church girls think that our only role in the "finding" process is sitting and waiting. A lot of us are hoping that we catch the attention of a suitable husband, and that the likelihood that we will be found by a good man is entirely up to that man. And Jesus. Jesus is going to make him find us. It feels like our choices are significantly limited to only the men who show interest in us.

> "Good ol' **church girls** think that our only role in the 'finding' process is **sitting and waiting.**"

I used to think that a great guy would randomly see me somewhere, and be so captivated by me that any other woman in the room would cease to exist. I would think, "I just need to keep doing what I'm doing, looking holy, and serving, and somebody would see me. I have a beautiful spirit, and a great personality—it's only a matter of time!"

Girl. I wish I could shake my former self! I would see plenty of handsome eligible men, and just think by osmosis they would come over to me and ask me out! It happens like that sometimes, but it's not a realistic expectation all the time! You know who would always approach me without hesitation? The guys I didn't like! I'm not talking about the guys women turn down who are actually really good men: I'm talking about the guys who are just imperfect in all of their ways! I knew that I had this whole "getting found" thing twisted and that I would need to be more strategic about receiving what I desired.

Ruth and Boaz

I talk about them a lot, I know. But there are so many overlooked principles in their story, and I get a new revelation every timed I read about them! The way that the story of Ruth and Boaz was presented to me was that Ruth was able to get the attention of Boaz because she was "working in her calling" and being a great daughter to her mother-in-law. The preachers would say, "Keep gleaning for Jesus, and the man that God has for you will find you." I don't disagree. I do believe that we need to walk in our callings, and do Kingdom work as singles. But that ain't completely how Ruth got a man. Mama Naomi instructed Ruth on how she needed to present herself in order to get Boaz's attention:

Wash therefore and anoint yourself, and put on your cloak and go down to the threshing floor, but do not make yourself known to the man until he has finished eating and drinking. But when he lies down, observe the place where he lies. Then go and uncover his feet and lie down, and he will tell you what to do."
(Ruth 3:3-4)

Look Good

Now, here's what I noticed about the advice Naomi gave. First, she told Ruth to wash herself, put on some perfume (anoint yourself), and put on some nice clothes (put on your cloak). I hope I don't have to explain this one too much! Look good, hunny! Slay! You can't expect to catch eyes with the guy you are attracted to if you don't take pride in the way that you look. It's okay to throw a little mascara on and put a little color on your lips. It doesn't make you a jezebel, I promise! Yea, I know. We've been told that beauty is in the eye of the beholder and that it's the inside that really counts—but we cannot ignore how big physical attraction is! Don't get it confused though: the physical is what attracts, but you have to have some substance in order to maintain the interest!

Position Yourself

See, Mama Naomi knew that it was more to this whole thing than just looking good. She told Ruth to strategically place herself in a position to be seen by Boaz. Now, I want to emphasize something very important here: this was not a sexual advance. Ruth was not instructed to throw herself at Boaz or attempt to seduce him. As a matter of fact, this was a custom that was well observed among this culture.

Which brings us to present day. Position yourself in places that have the potential to house the men that you want to meet! It might not always be the church! If you like intellectual men, go to the library, or a museum, or a play. If you'll have none of that, then go to some concerts, a monster truck show—somewhere! Take a class, start a new hobby. Really, this is an invitation to live life. Available men are everywhere, so get your fine self together and go out and be seen!

Make Your Intentions Known

So Ruth was there, on Boaz's floor, looking good and smelling good. She had done well with her mother's advice, but it was what she said to him that really made the story interesting! She said, "Spread your wings over me." Another translation says, "Take me under your protective wing." Homegirl was not playing about making sure that Boaz knew her intentions! Of course, we read the story and we know that he marries her, but I want to take the time to discuss what we can learn about Ruth and her presentation to Boaz.

Now this, I will admit, will mess with a lot of you. Hey, it's still a little uncomfortable for me! It's very bothersome because a lot of us have been taught to let the man make the first "move" or initiate the conversation. I was even under the impression that it was best to pretend that you didn't like the man at all or that you've never paid him any attention! I can't even pin-point the source of that ideology, but that is wack! It doesn't even make sense! It's okay to let a man know that you are interested! There is, however, a very fine line between letting your intentions be known and chasing after the man. I've give you two examples from my personal life.

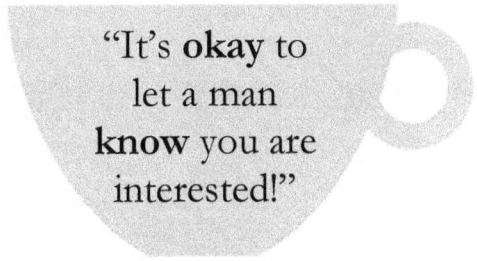

> "It's **okay** to let a man **know** you are interested!"

I was at an event, and I had a friendly conversation with a man who was there. We jumped from topic to topic, discussed our vocations and family life—nothing seemed forced at all. By the end of the night, I was sure that I wanted to talk to him again. The old me would have waited and wondered if he was interested. I decided to take a chance. We both were at the event in a professional capacity, so I didn't think it was proper to be trying to "mack" while I was there. After the event was over, I sent him a message that simply said, "I really enjoyed our conversation tonight. I would love to continue it in a more personal setting." I wasn't overly flirtatious (though I'm not against flirting!), I made sure that he perceived me as a woman of class.

After I sent my message, the guy did express mutual interest, and it wasn't long before we started to go on regular dates and learn more about each other. If you do this, there is something that you must—and I mean must—understand. The ball is now completely in his court. You're not going to pursue anything, you're going to give him the opportunity to do so.

If you have ego issues, then this will be the most uncomfortable thing in the world, because there is the possibility that the guy could decline! If he is interested, he will follow up with you and make the initiative to see you again. You won't need to pick the day, double check his availability, or plan the date. He should now act on his interest in you! If he's a little unenthusiastic

The Art of Flirting

Christian women, don't be afraid of flirting! It's a tool that we have in our arsenal that can be very beneficial if used correctly! Flirting looks very different depending on the woman: some play with their hair, some laugh and giggle a lot (guilty), some use their body language—but the main goal of flirting is to let a man know that you are interested without being overt or explicit. Though there is a way to be tastefully overt, flirting is a more delicate and charming way to project your feminine aura. It's a way to draw a man in—sometimes even without his permission! Flirting gives him that lingering thought, "Was she really interested in me, or was she just being friendly?" The thought alone could be enough to spark an interest.

Here's what makes flirting an art: it has to be done in a what that is not sexually suggestive or desperate! We're not seducing anyone! Sure, the world might show us a woman teasing her straw with her tongue or "carelessly" placing her hand on the guy's leg, but that's not the image that we as Christian women want to project. So, it's time to brush up on your flirting skills! Tap into your inner confidence and splendor, and start projecting your dopeness!

in his pursuit, then take it to mean that he is not interested. Do not try to force a connection, and don't chase him.

There was another situation, however, that didn't really pan out as successfully as I had hoped. My dad sent me on a mission to retrieve some auto equipment so that he could work on my truck, and I was reunited with someone I hadn't seen in years! Time had done him well! He looked better than he did the last time I saw him nearly ten years prior. We caught up and talked about the details of our present lives. He seemed to be in a really good place. I made another trip to the store, and he was there again, smiling and grinning at me. We talked outside while he helped me fix an issue with my vehicle, and I very casually suggested that we catch up over lunch soon. He said that it was a great idea, and locked my number in his phone. I never heard from him.

Because I do have a bit of an ego issue, I was a little unnerved that he didn't call me, especially considering how good I was looking that day, too! I wasn't going to call him and remind him about lunch: I am a beautiful woman who gave him an invitation to pursue me! I don't require a reminder because I'm hard to forget! I brought my offense into perspective: I'm opening myself up more to the possibility of meeting the person who is suitable for me because I'm no longer standing against the wall hoping that someone will approach me.

So I'll say this: get over the idea that the fate of your love life is in the hands of someone else! God has given us the ability to choose who we want to be with, although we need to seek Him and be discerning when we're making those choices. God has graced us with awesome "woman-powers" that we have to our advantage! Now, because I don't want y'all pastors to dog me in the pulpit, I will reiterate that it is not our place to pursue or persuade a man to be with us. What we can do, however, is at least put some bait on the line!

I adjure you, O daughters of Jerusalem,
by the gazelles or the does of the field,
that you not stir up or awaken love
until it pleases.
(Song of Solomon 3:5)

Be Done with It...

1. What has challenged or changed your understanding of being found or being pursued by a man?

2. Are you comfortable with "flirting"? Does flirting come naturally to you or do you need to gradually work flirting into your repertoire?

3. If your desire is to explore the dating scene, what could you do differently that you hadn't done previously? What new places could you explore in order to meet men who share some of your interests?

chapter 7

I'm So Over

Rejection

Whether you place yourself in a position to be pursued by a man, or if he initiates the pursuit, it kind of sucks when you've experienced rejection for any reason. Rejection (if you let it) has a nasty habit of magnifying your insecurities and assassinating your confidence. Once you've been rejected a couple of times, it's hard not to wonder if there's something wrong with you!

I have been rejected before, but in some situations I was more upset that the guy wasn't upfront with me about how he really felt than the actual rejection. I've had some men coward out those conversations to just leave me wondering what went wrong. Sometimes people reject with their inconsistencies; such was the situation with a particular man I met a season or two in the past.

Kierra C. Jones

No Southern Hospitality

Let me tell you that this was a beautiful man who stood at a majestic 6'3". He eyes looked like they could see into your innermost wonderings, and he had charming southern drawl that I adored. I was already imagining the tall babies I was planning on having with this man, and how I'd be sitting on my porch sipping sweet tea watching him cutting the grass. Ha! Not only was he physical perfection, he was also an ordained minister! This was huge for me because I value having a partner who not only shares my same faith, but who is also spiritually compatible with me. He had a very lucrative career, no ex-wives or baby mamas. To the Lord, again, I pounded my chest and threw the peace sign. I thought the Lord was looking out for me with this one!

I smiled and blushed reading all of the compliments he'd given me through text and social media. I couldn't wait to talk to him in person. He didn't make the whole "I met you on Facebook" thing seem weird: I was very comfortable with the idea of getting to know him. When we were finally able to have an evening of Facetime, I was blown away by our connection and general agreeability. He was interested in marriage and had shared that he was actively looking for a wife. The conversation was very intriguing and he answered every question I asked him perfectly. We were textbook compatible. He lived out of state, which was a drawback, but homeboy said that his job afforded him the opportunity to relocate. He said he would have no problem doing that for the right woman! I was too giddy and optimistic about this possibility.

I was in fairytale land for a while, but eventually things began to fall off. After our first conversation, he texted me and told me how much he enjoyed talking to me. We planned to talk again the next evening. I preferred to call him since I knew that my daughter would probably make bedtime challenging. I made sure that I

72

looked "effortlessly" cute—you know, when you try to make it look like you really didn't try but you actually did. I was ready for our video chat. I called and he didn't answer. I didn't sweat it; I assumed he would call back when he was available. Another hour went by, and I so happened to see that he was currently active on Facebook. "Hmmm," I thought, "If he's active on Facebook, then surely he saw my call." I kept it cool. I sent him a cute little message on Facebook messenger telling him that I hope we'd be able to talk. He didn't respond, but Facebook told me that he saw my message (FB is so messy).

"If he's **active** on Facebook, then surely **he saw** my call!"

I was a bit confused, but I gave him the benefit of the doubt. Hey, we're grown right? We have lives; should I expect for him to be rearranging his evening to speak to me? The next day he came up with some excuse as to why he wasn't able to talk. I wasn't buying it, but I said that I would give him another chance. As a matter of fact, I told him that he could call me this time. I was sure that there had to be some misunderstanding and that I'd be a "Petty Betty" for dismissing him because of mixed communication. *The same thing happened again.* He was online, but he didn't call. By now I'm thinking that he's playing games, for which I had no time. I kid you not, he texted me the next day like nothing was wrong. Of course, I communicated how confused I was and how I was looking forward to speaking to him. He seemed completely confused. I told him that if he was interested in me like he said, calling me would not be an issue. He agreed and promised that he'd do better. Y'all wouldn't believe me if I told y'all that he didn't call.

I was over it. I may not have a Ph.D., but I can tell when

somebody's just not that in to me. It wasn't my thing to beg someone to talk to or get to know me, so I wasn't going to press the issue any longer. It was clear that for whatever reason he was rejecting me, so I decided to fall back with my dignity still intact.

No Thanks, Elder!

So, you know it's something when an elder from your church decides that he wants to hook you up. It's something entirely extreme when he tells you that he already sent the guy your picture and your bio! I was mortified. I didn't think I looked that lowly and depressed without a man that someone would feel the need to play cupid! In any case, after I crucified this elder for trying to set me up, I at least agreed to see what this guy he was matching me with was all about.

> "I can tell when somebody's **just not that in to me!**

The first conversation that we had was awesome. We laughed about a few things, had some great stories to exchange, and we even poked fun at the elder who attempted to set us up. This guy was a BMW (black man working), owned his home, was active in church, and was that rugged kind of handsome that I appreciated. In the weeks to follow we texted back and forth, had a few more conversations, and really enjoyed getting to know each other. Then the phone calls weren't as often on his end. The text replies took longer and longer. I didn't want to seem thirsty so I didn't have a cow over the change in communication, but I did let him know that I noticed it. Eventually, he asked me if I would like to go out. I agreed, and I was excited because I thought that he had great potential.

He. Stood. Me. Up. The day that we were supposed to go out,

I'm So Over It

I made sure that my hair, makeup and outfit was on point. Then I texted him to make sure that we were still on. Nothing. After an hour had passed, I called him and was sent to voicemail. I figured that something was up, but I didn't think that he would just ignore me after he'd been the one to suggest the date. In any case, I figured that he would just call me the next day with an apology and an explanation. He didn't.

The next time that I saw him, he was walking hand in hand with a beautiful woman and gazing lovingly into her eyes. They looked so good together. I was pissed. This wasn't a new relationship: she was in the picture all along. He at least owed me the decency of telling me that they were trying to work things out so that I didn't waste my time. My ego was bruised terribly. I already wasn't keen on the fact that an elder decided that I needed help with my love life. I also wasn't keen on the fact that the guy that I was "hooked up with" played my entire life!

But this experience was so necessary to my growth and development. If nothing else, I learned that I'm not for everyone. I'm not everyone's "it." I'm not the woman that every man has been praying for and dreaming about. It seems so vain to have to even realize that, but I did. There is no doubt about it: I am an amazing woman, and I don't think that I'm the only one who thinks so. As a matter of fact, my "Key-hive" was getting ready to let this guy have it after I told them how he had stood me up and dated another woman! If I interact with each man like I'm the answer to his prayers, then I'm setting myself up for ego-crushing if he decides that I may not be his cup of Kool-Aid. Granted, based on how we were affiliated, I thought that the decent thing to do would have been to at least cancel the date. Later it would have been good to have a conversation with me about not wanting to pursue things any further. I had to see him every Sunday after that, and not once did he explain himself!

It is okay for someone to decide not to be with you. Everyone has a right to choose who they want. Unless they have entered into a covenant relationship with you, everyone isn't entitled to journey with you. What's not okay is someone being manipulative and dishonest about their intentions with you. I think we all deserve that "this probably isn't going to work" conversation in the least bit.

Boaz, Not "Yoaz"

Let's dip back into the book of Ruth. There is yet another lesson to be learned! I've already discussed how Ruth won the affections of Boaz and lived biblically happily ever after. The story of Ruth and Boaz was taught so well that at one point all single Christian women were "waiting on Boaz." I was even tempted to buy a t-shirt that said "Waiting on Boaz, Not Yoaz"! Ha! As I read the story of Ruth and Boaz another time, I realized that there was another important character who is often overlooked. It wasn't Naomi or Ruth's mother-in-law—no, it was that nameless kinsman in the second chapter.

After Ruth's whole "threshing floor" demonstration, Boaz was sure that he wanted to marry Ruth. The only problem is that there was someone standing between him and his wedded bliss. According to the law, there was a closer kinsman who was entitled to marry Ruth, and if that kinsman agreed to take Ruth as his wife, Boaz would not have the right to claim Ruth.

To move the story along a little bit, this kinsman decided that he didn't want Ruth. He didn't want to be with this amazing, compassionate, humble, loyal, beautiful, hard-working woman. In all of her splendor and majesty, he was okay with passing up the opportunity to make her his own. One could say that Ruth had been rejected! But what didn't work for that man worked perfectly for Boaz. I can imagine his step having a little skip in it once he got word that he was able to marry Ruth!

Think about it: Ruth could have been thoroughly offended that this "kinsman" didn't want her. I'm using my imagination here a bit with Ruth, but some of us have to change the way that we view rejection. There was a man willing to be exactly who and what Ruth needed, but had another man not rejected her, she wouldn't have been in the position to be blessed with Boaz. Some of us need to be denied who we think we want so that we can be in proper position for who is right for us. What I also find interesting about Ruth's marriage to Boaz is the fact that there was a special assignment on

"Some of us need to be denied who we **think** we want..."

their union. They are a part of Christ's lineage. They birthed some of the greatest game-changers in history! Had Ruth married someone else, she wouldn't have taken part in paving the way for our Lord and Savior.

Rejected but Not Abandoned

Another rejected woman in the Bible was Hagar, Sarah's handmaiden. She really didn't have a choice but to have sex with Abraham because Sarah had instructed her to do so. The interesting part was that after Hagar had performed her servantly "duties" and bore Abraham a son, Sarah had the nerve to demand that Hagar and her son, Ishmael, be exiled from the land! Remember, it was Sarah's idea for Hagar to even get pregnant by Abraham in the first place!

Even in her rejection, God's hand was still on Hagar's life. She fled to the dessert and thought that she and her son would die of thirst, but the Lord made provision for them. They lacked nothing. Ishmael grew strong in might and seeded a mighty nation!

I love this story because even though Hagar and Ishmael were not a part of the plan that God had for Abraham and Sarah's life, He still set them on a path to their own blessings! Hagar's rejection was not her undoing!

Just because you were rejected by a man, it doesn't mean that your world has to come crashing down! It doesn't mean that you are any less wonderful. Some people simply don't align with the assignment that is on our lives, and sometimes we don't align with theirs. That's okay. There is still provision for you! In any case, I'm grateful for the denials and the rejections—I just need for the elders to be praying a little harder next time they decide to send someone my way!

But you, Israel, my servant, Jacob, whom I have chosen, the offspring of Abraham, my friend; you whom I took from the ends of the earth, and called from its farthest corners, saying to you, "You are my servant, I have chosen you and not cast you off...".
(Isaiah 41:8-9)

Be Done with It...

1. Have you ever been rejected by someone? How could that rejection place you in a position to receive a blessing?

2. Recount a time when being rejected has caused you to experience growth and self-reflection.

chapter 8

I'm So Over

Not Being Good Enough

We all have our hang-ups about ourselves, but at what point do hang-ups become debilitating insecurities? I believe it happens when we allow them to overshadow the wonderful individuals that we are. When we allow our flaws to hinder rather than challenge us. I have spent my entire life trying to fix things I thought were wrong with me, and I never cared to focus on the things that were actually right with me. It has been a chore for sure, but I had to get over years of thinking that I wasn't good enough.

So, I'm a little on the thick side. Okay, on that needle of "little thick" and "lotta thick," I'm more like halfway. At least in my mind. Most of my life I had been heavier than the other girls around me, but that didn't stop me from getting plenty of attention from boys and men. Actually, it was the reason why I measured my worth based on how men perceived me.

As an adult, my weight became more of a concern to me. Honestly, I didn't care about being healthy more than I cared about looking good. If I was 145 pounds with sugar diabetes I would be alright as long as I could slay in a body-con dress. Sad, I know, but that's the struggle that I had to overcome.

I'm not so sure how I came to hate my body, but I'm sure that the media had its hand in how I perceived myself. I came to revere those small-waisted hourglass goddesses who pranced around the screen and the internet—no matter how photoshopped or surgically enhanced they were. I felt like guys liked this type of body shape best, and so when I looked at my full-waisted regular-bootied body, I saw someone who was not physically desirable.

And that became an issue. I only saw my body as a tool to attract men. Don't get me wrong, I did want to look good physically just for my own sake, but when it came down to it, I wanted to make men's heads turn. In fact, I was so influenced by how attractive I was to men that when one guy told me that he liked women with big butts, I was doing squats and leg presses like a mad woman. I was about to give Serena Williams a run for her money! What's crazy is that plenty of men have told me that they actually loved my body and that it was sexy, but I wouldn't hear it. I would refute their statements, pointing out something unattractive about my body. That was an extremely annoying habit of mine.

I looked to **men** to **validate me** because I didn't know how to validate **myself.**

I also discovered that the way I felt about myself was manifested in the type of men that I entertained and how I entertained them. I was an insecure hot mess so I would endure a lot of garbage and make unhealthy compromises. I looked to men to validate me because I didn't know how to validate myself. I wanted men to give me value because I also didn't have an intrinsic appreciation of myself.

I Can't Do Any Better

I look back and shudder at the times that I would get driven through the mud trying to hold on to a man who clearly wasn't the best choice for me. It was because I believed the lie that he was the best that I had been with and that I probably couldn't do any better. Case and point: I met someone who was intelligent, financially stable, extremely handsome, and college educated. I was in awe of the many things that he had accomplished—so much that I wanted to be around him just to hear him talk.

Eventually, things went awry, and he told me that he wasn't looking to have the type of relationship that I desired, even though he liked me very much. Now, the normal response would be to respect his decision and move on like the elegant confident lady that I am now, but no. No, no, no. My mind had convinced me that there would never be another man like him. My mind kept reminding me how I had never dated anyone with a Master's Degree before or someone who was so driven and devoted to achieving success. I glorified everything that he was and downplayed everything that he was not. I decided that I couldn't let this one get away. What were the chances that I'd find someone who was better than him?

The problem with this way of thinking was that in my exaltation of this man, I began to compromise a lot of what I wanted and what I expected from him. I was attempting to meet him halfway on some of the issues that we were having while dating, but he wasn't willing to budge. Because I was so convinced that he was the best thing walking in chocolate skin, I gave him all of the leverage in the relationship. I found myself allowing things that I definitely shouldn't have allowed all in the name of "not letting this good man get away." The ball was completely in his court, and he wasn't even trying to play the game!

A mental shift was in order. First, I had to think about how many times I had "fallen in love" with someone and thought that I'd never find anyone greater. Unfortunately, it happened all the time! I am such a sappy romantic that I was making Shakespearean declarations like I was written into the script of Romeo and Juliet. I just knew that I'd lost the best thing that ever happened to me—that is until the next "great" man came along.

Although I don't believe that it is healthy to jump from relationship to relationship or to anticipate catching man after man, the reality is that great men are in abundance! I am a great woman, so I don't have to settle! Why put so much energy into trying to hold onto a man who doesn't need to be held onto? I can just let him go! Why would I buy into the myth that I'm not good enough to be on the arm of a wonderful man? Truth be told, I am great whether a man is in my life or if he isn't!

Damaged Goods

I know plenty women who also feel like they aren't "worthy" of a good man because of decisions they've made in the past regarding their sexuality. Some women might feel that because they've had multiple sexual partners in the past, a "good man" wouldn't even want them. What's shocking to me is that many Christian women actually feel this way—even after knowing that their sins have been forgiven through Christ!

There are plenty of women in the Bible who have dealt in some form of sexual deviance, but the important thing is that when those women had an encounter with God, they were forever changed. One woman was actually caught in the middle of "getting it in" when she came into contact with Jesus:

The scribes and the Pharisees brought a woman who had been caught in adultery, and placing her in the midst they said to him, "Teacher, this woman has been caught in the act of adultery. Now in the Law Moses commanded us to stone such women. So what do you say?" This they said to test him, that they might have some charge to bring against him. Jesus bent down and wrote with his finger on the ground. And as they continued to ask him, he stood up and said to them, "Let him who is without sin among you be the first to throw a stone at her." And once more he bent down and wrote on the ground. But when they heard it, they went away one by one, beginning with the older ones, and Jesus was left alone with the woman standing before him. Jesus stood up and said to her, "Woman, where are they? Has no one condemned you?" She said, "No one, Lord." And Jesus said,"Neither do I condemn you; go, and from now on sin no more."

(John 8:1-11)

Did I tell you how much I love Jesus? The scribes and Pharisees were always trying to find a way to trip Jesus up, but they were never ready for his responses! What I love about this passage is the fact that those who were so ready to condemn this adulterous woman had to first examine themselves. They were so ready to justify this woman's death without even considering the sin that each of them had in their own lives.

I believe that a man who loves God and is living according to the word of God will accept your past, celebrate your present, and be excited about your future. I believe that such a man knows how lost and hopeless we all were without Christ, and he can even acknowledge his own mistakes and shortcomings. If you are a woman of God boldly walking in liberty and deliverance, the light that is in you will no doubt blot out the darkness that was once in your past. A true man of God would be able to appreciate your shine!

> "**Accept** your past, **celebrate** your present, and **be excited** about your future!"

Although my past was definitely sprinkled with dirt, I can honestly say that once I allowed God to heal and deliver me from my sexual sin, I no longer viewed myself as damaged goods. I could have let my mind entertain thoughts of unworthiness, but I remembered that in Christ I am a new creature! I had to remember that he shed his blood for me on Calvary, and as a result, my past can no longer hold me hostage. You have to have that same confidence. Do not let the devil convince you that you aren't as good as the next woman because of what you've done before coming into the full knowledge of Christ. We all were born into sin, and we all need Christ to operate as the propitiation for our sins!

Who Told You That?

In the Bible, when Adam and Eve ate from the tree of knowledge, their eyes were opened and they learned of their nakedness. In response to their new knowledge, they sewed leaves together to hide their "shame". When they explained to God why they were hiding, God asked, "Who told you that you were naked (Genesis 3:11)?" Immediately, I looked at myself and heard some questions asked to me in my perception of God's voice:

Who told you that you weren't beautiful?
Who told you that you weren't worthy?
Who told you that you were worthless?
Who told you to hate your body?

And my answer had to be similar to what Eve told God: "The serpent deceived me (Genesis 3:13)." The "serpent" or the enemy has done an awesome job at making many of us believe that we are less than fearfully and wonderfully made. Sometimes we've internalized things that others have said about us so much that negative thoughts have taken root in our mind.

I'm now in the process of loving me. It's a sloppy messy journey, but one that I'm enduring with positivity. I'm not going to front and act like one day I'll go to the mirror and be like, "Oh, how I love the way my gut sags over my pants!" If you know me personally, please slap me if I ever say that. For me, it's more about loving who am I now even in the midst of striving to be better. It's about me wanting to improve my physical appearance or anything else that I don't like about me simply because I want to. I want to do it so that I like what I see. It's about me making the disconnection that a slimmer more shapely body means a better man. I'm done with feeling less confident in the presence of a woman with a banging body. I'm so over it.

What I have done now is pick out particular things that I like about my body. I love my boobs. They are massive, but they give me a feminine softness. They are a life force; they nursed a little premature baby into full health. I also love the meat in my thighs and the way that my booty can fill up some jeans! I like how my shoulders look in a strapless or halter top dress. I like how even and smooth my skin is. I have a woman's body! Though it might not be ideal for me right now, I can still werk a room, hunny!

Affirmations in Your Birthday Suit!

If you are really battling with low self-esteem or any feelings of inadequacy do this exercise:

Stand in front of a full length mirror—naked. Yes, naked. Don't have on a stitch of clothing! Look at your body carefully. Focus on every bodypart, every scar, every stretch mark—really look at everything. Then start to say why you are beautiful. Start to talk about the things you deserve and what you do not deserve. Mention the things that you will do for yourself because you are deserving of love. Declare that you love yourself no matter your flaws and insecurities. Repeat this exercise daily. The first time you do it, you might feel uncomfortable. You might not even believe the things you are saying, but it's important that you confess these positive things about youself because the Bible says, "Life and death are in the power of the tongue." You have the power to create and change things based on what you confess. If it helps, write down what you're going to say ahead of time so that you can rehearse the same affirmations over and over again. Now loose your threads, and hop to it!

But I'm more than just the physical! I have a never ending reservoir of love, I am a God-chaser, I am creative, electrifying, and sensational! But I don't boast in and of myself—I am none of these without the Christ who dwells in me! How dare I discount all of the deposits He has made in me simply because I don't have a smaller number on the tags of my clothes!

Change Your Stinkin' Thinkin'

For some women, weight might not be something that is a personal hindrance. In the African American community, sometimes women can feel inferior because of a darker skin color or a kinkier texture of hair. I've definitely witnessed that in my own family, at work, and even within my circle of friends. I had one friend growing up who had the prettiest chocolate skin, but she was convinced that she was ugly because of it. She even had the goal of marrying a light skinned man so that her children would not be dark like her. It broke my heart that she thought that way!

We have to heal from such terrible way of thinking. Proverbs 23:7 says, *"As a man thinketh in his heart, so is he."* I dare to say that whatever a woman thinks and says about herself she will definitely become. Stop calling yourself ugly, or fat, or gumpy, or whatever it is that you've attached to yourself. Change that conversation so that you empower yourself. The Bible also says, *"Death and Life are in the power of the tongue, and they that love it shall eat the fruit thereof* (Proverbs 18:21)." Sow good fruit into yourself! Call yourself beautiful, and charming, and elegant, and unique, wonderful—and everything else great about you. Don't let yourself be limited to your physical appearance. Get over that.

If there is something that you can do to help you feel better about you (within reason, of course) then do it. If you feel like your hair is mediocre, take care of it! Find out what type of products work best for your hair type. If you hate your acne, invest in a good acne treatment product. If you hate the extra pounds that you've been carrying around, invest in a membership at a gym. Just promise me this: whatever you do, do it with the mindset that you are enhancing yourself. Don't try to make all of these alterations because you think you're not enough.

You are altogether beautiful, my love; there is no flaw in you.
(Song of Solomon 4:7)

Be Done with It...

1. What are some things that you love about yourself?

2. What are some things that you don't love about yourself? How could you change the way you think about those specific attributes so that you have a more positive sense of self?

chapter 9

I'm So Over

Parenting and Dating

When I had my daughter, I figured that I wouldn't be able to seriously date anyone until she was probably a teenager. I felt that she required and deserved so much from me, and that it was my fault she had been born into a single-parent home anyway. How dare I even think about dividing my attention between her and someone else? I am a mom. I couldn't possibly take on the role as someone's girlfriend, "bae," or whatever when there were so many "momly" things I felt that I should be tending to. Instead of getting my nails done in preparation for a date, I could've been buying Kasey something that would enhance her education. I would even feel guilty about asking my mom or grandmother to watch her so that I could smile and grin in some man's face. I didn't want to place the burden of my love life on others. I didn't think that it would be fair to Kasey to spend time with someone else when the time I already had with her was divided between her dad and me.

"I didn't want to place the **burden** of my **love-life** on others."

And speaking of her dad, I didn't want to even ask him to keep her so that I could go out on a date. He never gave me a reason to think that he'd have a problem with me dating someone else (not that I need his permission), but I was uncomfortable with the thought of him being on daddy duty while I was getting my groove back. I wouldn't have a problem if he dated someone else, and I didn't want to rekindle a relationship with him, so I didn't know why I felt so strange about him knowing about me dating. I didn't know why I felt odd about him making accommodations so that I could date either.

For a split second, I carried the belief that the kind of man that I wanted would have to be altered because I had already had a child. I thought that I'd have to settle because the "good men" don't want any women with kids. I thought they'd pass me right on by. I just knew that they would grow impatient with me having to plan things around the times that Kasey would be with her dad, or that I couldn't just up and do something spontaneous because I'd have to make sure that I had given a sitter (a.k.a. "my mama") enough time in advance to keep my daughter. I even asked one guy if he didn't mind if my daughter came with us to the movies! As you could imagine, he wasn't feeling that.

Loving Kasey

And then there was the huge question: could a man truly love my daughter as his own? I often think of all the horror stories about stepfathers abusing their stepchildren or taking advantage of them in the foulest of ways. I began immediately planning how I could get away with killing someone for hurting my baby. When I look at my child, my heart wells up with joy and I thank God for every moment that I have with her. I see this beautiful, intelligent, radiant little girl, and I wonder if any man besides her father could ever look upon her with the same type of awe. It scared me to even think that any man could profess to love me and not have the same conviction that I have to provide for, protect, and love her. I was afraid that I could love a man who didn't love my daughter, and I could not risk my responsibility to her for the sake of him.

> "I was afraid that I could love a man who **didn't love** my daughter."

No Baby-Daddies, Please!

Then I was thinking: all the "good men" probably have this perception that I'm in constant drama with my child's father or that I'm still in love with him. Someone even told me that the child's father would always be a threat to the new relationship because he'll always hold a special place in the woman's life! I was told that a "good man" didn't have time for this, and would much rather find a woman who was childless with flexible availability. I was under the impression that a man's dream is to start a family with his own seed, and that a ready-made family was not his ideal. I didn't want any friction between a future husband and Kasey's father.

Love or Custody?

What if my potential husband wanted to move out of state? What if he got an awesome job opportunity that required us to move a significant distance from where we currently reside? I would not be able to move out state with Kasey unless her father agreed—and he wouldn't. I wouldn't even want her to be away from her father. Even if we agreed to a specific custody agreement, I wouldn't want to be away from my baby either. Would I be bound to be within "x" number of miles from Kasey's dad until she turned eighteen? What a fate! Would a potential husband even understand the feelings that I have or the reality of the co-parenting relationship that I have with Kasey's dad? I resolved that it is much easier not date and parent at the same time because I didn't want to have to juggle all of these complex emotions and try to experience love at the same time.

Biblical Blended Family

Then I read my Bible (cue the organ)! Mary and Joseph were a part of a "blended family"! Yes, Jesus Himself had a stepfather! Joseph was a step-daddy! It's easy to miss something like this when you've heard the story of Jesus's birth so many times. Honestly, it would have never occurred to me to view Mary and Joseph in this light until I created a situation that would place me in a blended family.

What's crazy to me is that Joseph felt the same way that many modern men feel about marrying women with children. Joseph was betrothed to Mary, but once he found out that she was pregnant, he was about to bid her adieu (Matthew 1:19). Obviously, the situation was a little different because she was the only woman in the world to have been impregnated by the Holy Spirit, but what happens next reveals an entire world of revelation.

> *But after he had considered this* (divorcing Mary), *an angel of the Lord appeared to him in a dream and said, "Joseph son of David, do not be afraid to take Mary home as your wife, because what is conceived in her is from the Holy Spirit.*
>
> (Matthew 1:20)

Joseph listened to God and took Mary as his wife. I believe that just as God spoke to Joseph about the rewarding responsibility of caring for a child that wasn't his biologically, He can also do that for the man who is right for me—and for you if we happen to be in the same predicament. I commend Joseph for even trusting God enough to stay with Mary. The average man would not have been able to handle raising someone else's child. He must have been a man of great compassion, understanding, love, and support—qualities that make for a great father!

What's also interesting to me is that the angel says, "What's conceived in her is of the Holy Spirit." Because of my connection with God, there are so many wonderful things on the inside of me that are getting ready to come forth! My gifts, talents, anointing, and favor are still being incubated by the Holy Spirit. I'm ready to pop! Guess what? That's not just for me, it's also for the man who will be in covenant with me. Though I had a child out of wedlock and had to deal with the consequences of that decision, my destiny is grand; I am in a great position to be a consistently flowing fountain of blessings for my

> "My gifts, talents, anointing, and favor are still being incubated by the Holy Spirit."

Mommy Affirmations

♥ I am a beautiful and amazing woman; my child does not change those facts.

♥ There is a man is willing to love me and willing to love my child as his own.

♥ Being a single mother does not mean that I am not worthy of a good man or that I need to settle in my expectations of men.

♥ I am equipped to deal with any issues that may arise in a blended family, and God will give me the wisdom to do what is best for my family.

♥ Being a mother does not diminish my value, if anything, it enhances it.

♥ I have faith that God favors me and that all things will work together for my good.

household! If any man decides to pass me up because of my beautiful daughter, he will miss out on life more abundantly for sure!

Motherhood to Wifehood

I used to bash myself for becoming an unwed mother, but I appreciate what motherhood has taught me in my preparation for "wifehood". For one, I have learned how to sacrifice for the greater good of my home. This includes everything from my finances to my time: I've learned that the people in my household must come first. It was uncomfortable at first to say "no" to things and people that would have previously received a "yes" before Kasey. I can no longer think in terms of "me" but in "we". I am confident that this is a mindset that will serve me well in marriage.

As a mother, I've also learned that I have to put aside how I may feel at the moment to truly love those in my home. I have to be careful how I speak to Kasey even in my anger. Instead of being quick to assume or be angry, I must seek to understand. I must seek God in the things that I don't understand. I can imagine that there will be times when I am upset with my husband or times that I just don't understand what to do. I've learned how essential it is to cover those that I love in prayer and to truly love unconditionally. I've had a head start committing to enhancing these things into my life, and I can't wait to perfect them with my husband!

— · — · — · —

I'm learning that I have to let go of all of the reservations that I've had about dating and loving someone as a mother. I can't say for sure that I have a solution to all of the feelings and scenarios that I've just talked about, but I will say this: I trust God. In trusting Him, I have decided to give all of my apprehension and fear to Him because I know that He has a wonderful plan for me! I won't worry about the logistics of the how and why of my dating life because I have chosen to delight myself Christ first!

Again, we must not forget that death and life is in the power of the tongue! We can be proactive in speaking against any of those negative thoughts that pertain to dating and marrying as a single mother. I refuse to let my own negative thoughts block me from experiencing God's richest blessings!

Don't be discouraged if you are a single mother. I believe that the man who is suitable for you will love you and your child as his own. He will not view you as damaged goods, but will appreciate your journey and the woman you have become because of it. Now, don't bash the brothers who prefer not to be with someone who is already a mother. People have their preferences. I even have mine. But don't feel like you are ineligible for a good man because of your past. You are good enough for the right person for you. We are in Christ, He works things out for our good!

And we know that all things work together for good to them that love God, to them who are the called according to his purpose.
(Romans 8:28

Be Done with It...

1. If you are a single mother, what apprehensions do you have about dating again? How can you combat that negative thought with a positive affirmation?

2. Did you ever feel like you weren't eligible for a good man because you already had a child(ren)? What have you learned that challenges this old way of thinking?

chapter 10

I'm So Over

Competing with Women

When I was in the second grade, there was a girl in my class who was absolutely gorgeous—even with her two front teeth missing. As adults, we reconnected and she is just as gorgeous as I remembered her. She had pretty brown skin, big baby doll eyes, and long silky hair. Really, it was the hair that I especially loved. I was raised to think that the longer your hair was the prettier you were—her hair was longer than mine, so I applied the "rule" and concluded that she must have been prettier than me. The problem was that little second grade me recognized how beautiful she was, and I became extremely jealous of her. In fact, one day out of the blue, I told one of my friends to go over and hit her. I would have done it myself, but I was such a "good girl" that I couldn't possibly carry it out. Well my little friend, Bianca, was "about that life;" she went over to the pretty girl (who we'll call De-De) and slapped her as hard as she could. Of course De-De was shocked that my friend had hit her, and I even heard her ask Bianca why she did it. Bianca simply pointed to me and said, "She told me to do it."

De-De immediately went over to our teacher, and said, "Kierra told Bianca to hit me!" I was sick with conviction. I didn't want anything to happen that would make me get in trouble. My teacher reprimanded Bianca, of course, and then she came to me. "Why did you tell Bianca to hit De-De?" she asked, the disappointment evident in her voice.

I responded like a typical second-grader, "I don't know." Only I did know why. She threatened me. I allowed her beauty to make me question my own, and that made me feel inadequate around her. I didn't realize it back then, but I saw her as competition. I definitely was into boys even at that age, and in my tiny seven-year-old mind, I had to rationalize that if I thought she was beautiful, the boys must have thought so, too! The only way that I could process all of this was to be violent towards her—but by way of my "henchman," Bianca.

When I entered fourth grade, I had booty and boobs like a grown woman. The boys would snicker and point (because that's what fourth grade boys do when they're aroused apparently), and the girls would smack their lips and roll their eyes. Someone even coined the nickname "Water Balloons" because one of the girls in my class had spread a rumor that I had been filling my bra with water balloons every day.

Even as an adult, I couldn't quite shake the habit of becoming jealous of other women. This is after knowing Christ, being in ministry, and having a great career! I would look at other beautiful successful women and be secretly jealous of their ministries, businesses, and sometimes their beauty! And then, when these great women would become engaged and married, I would really feel green. Somehow, I allowed the enemy to convince me that such women were threats to me. I was convinced that they were my competition when it came to success and marriage. Obviously, these were great women; I figured that if I thought so, other available, attractive, successful, saved men would also be taking notice and not noticing me. I couldn't tell you all how I came to peace that theory together.

The Cost of Jealousy

Why do women seem to have this innate response to hate on other women who have it going on in one way or another? Why do we sometimes feel threatened by another bomb woman? Biology tells us that women have a prehistoric propensity to compete with each other because other women threatened access to the male's provisions. Basically, our ancestors didn't want to have to spread the food supply and other necessities amongst other women and the children that the men could possibly bring. Actually, that theory might not be too prehistoric at all considering how a family is affected when the husband steps out on his wife and creates other children. That family's provisions are now being affected by two words: child support!

The reality is that our jealousy of other women could take the focus off of our own assignment and hinder our own opportunities to be blessed. We can definitely understand this by examining the life of King Saul.

Saul was tall, fine, and strong—the favor of God was on his life. He had it going on, and he had the respect of the people he ruled. It's safe to say that he wasn't lacking in the confidence area—well that is until he met David. At first, Saul loved David. He had trusted many tasks to David and even let him rule over some of his armies. The problem arose when Saul saw how much favor David had with God and how much God's anointing was on David's life. As a result, Saul was so jealous of David that he had his heart set on David's demise. He tried time and time again to kill David but was unsuccessful because, again, God's favor was on David's life! (1 Samuel 19)

What's interesting to me is that the reason David even came into the picture in the first place was because Saul was disobedient to God. He let his position and his own pride take priority over his relationship with God. Many times we can become envious of how God is blessing and elevating others when we ourselves are not even walking in obedience. We haven't followed God's instruction so that we can be blessed, too!

> "We haven't followed God's **instruction** so that we can be **blessed**, too!"

We allow the enemy to make us think that God loves or favors others more than us, but the reality is that God is not a respecter of person, He's a respecter of principle. You might look at "Sister So-and-So" and turn your nose up at her, but you don't know what she's sowed and sacrificed in order to be where she is today. Some women are jealous of women with great husbands, but won't follow God's word about abstaining from sexual immorality or demonstrating the attributes of a godly wife. Some are jealous of another woman's influence and endless opportunities but won't apply the principle of hardwork and discipline. Ouch.

> "What **things, opportunities, or relationships** are you killing because of your **jealousy?**"

Also keep in mind that good ol' King Saul became so obsessed with bringing King David down, that his death came at his own hand. What things, opportunities, or relationships are you killing because of your jealousy? Don't you know that when you are insecure and jealous, you give off negative energy? What if there was a great opportunity coming your way, but because you don't know how to applaud someone else, the spirit of "stankness" overshadowed you and you missed out? You could even meet a wonderful man and easily drive him away because you are too busy worrying about the next woman.

Getting Over Jealousy

One of the best ways that I learned to get over jealousy was to recognize and applaud my own assets and abilities. Can't nobody do it quite like Ki. Another woman might do an awesome job at ministering and speaking, but nobody can get a message across like I can. I'm nobody's carbon copy. And that's not to boast on myself, but it's me having confidence in the uniqueness that God bestowed upon me. No one else looks like me (well, except my Auntie Rita, but that's genetics). Nobody can rock a head full of locs like I can rock them. Nobody's style is quite like mine, nobody is creative like I'm creative. Nobody else's mind works the way mine does. My smile is like no other. And I could go on and on. I don't have to worry about competing with another woman especially when it comes to a man because I have full confidence that the person most suitable for me won't even want anybody else! And if his eyes did happen to observe another fabulous woman, I trust that he will remain a man of integrity.

Who are you? What's on the inside of you that makes you 100% authentic? There are some things that you can do that nobody else can. Realize that you were fearfully and wonderfully made! I used to be confused about why the Bible said that we are fearfully made and then I got this awesome revelation: God made each and every one of us so carefully and wonderfully because He feared making a mistake. He has made us complete. The more we cultivate our relationship with God, the more complete and great we become. Every potential for greatness is already in us. Our consistent walk with God is what causes that greatness to continually manifest. The only person who we should be in competition with is ourselves.

Celebrate Other Women

I know so many women who would rather drink poison than give another woman a compliment. In fact, I was having a conversation with one woman about how cute another woman's outfit was, and she just had to point out that it looked a couple of sizes too small.

I've mastered the art of complimenting women. I love to do it! It wasn't always in my culture to do so; I had to unlearn all of the catty ways that I grew up with and truly learn how to celebrate women. One time I was shopping, and I saw a woman who was gorgeous. The old me would have concluded that she "wasn't even that cute," but the new me could admire her. We were in the checkout line and I said, "Excuse me, I just wanted to tell you that you are so beautiful!" She thanked me, but it was written all over her face that she was uncomfortable with me complimenting her. I didn't take offense: I realize that many of us are so used to other women being jealous and catty that we don't know how to take a sincere compliment from another woman! Perhaps she didn't even think she that was beautiful. One of my friends even suggested that the woman may have thought that I was hitting on her, but my tone definitely didn't suggest that!

I believe that sowing compliments and words of encouragement not only builds up the receiving woman, but also ourselves. It's the simple principle (there's that word again) of sowing and reaping. When we sow positivity we also reap positivity. And if you know anything about sowing and reaping, you know that you always reap more than what you originally planted. Let's change the culture among women. Purpose in your mind today to uplift your follow woman if not for her sake, for your own at least!

Don't Envy, Learn

Ooh wee. I can sense that this one is going to mess with a few of you. Well, the few of you who are still holding on to your jealous habits. If you meet a woman and you're tempted with being jealous, redirect those feelings and figure out what you could learn from her in order to improve yourself! I'm so serious!

For example, instead of being jealous of that woman with that awesome successful business, ask her some tips for expanding your business! If you find yourself envying another woman's physique, ask her for some fitness tips and implement them! Tired of women getting engaged and married around you? Talk to them about their dating process and the standards and boundaries they established with their husbands. If jealousy is a big issue for you, this will no doubt mess with your pride. It may be hard for you to even acknowledge that a particular woman is doing something well because somehow that makes you doubt yourself. Abandon that thought! Now, of course you have to be discerning about what you decide to implement in your life and the type of counsel that you seek.

> "Figure out what you can **learn** from her in order **to improve yourself!**"

Keep in mind, sometimes we are jealous of other women who have attributes that we should not embody. In such cases, our task shouldn't be to learn from those women, but change our thinking about those characteristics. Don't be jealous of Susan because she can twerk like a pro. The attention that she might get from twerking is not the same type of attention that you want. We have to change the way we view certain attributes!

She Tried It

If you're tempted to compete over a man, don't. Again, I say, "Don't." Please do not try to "one up" the next woman for the sake of a man! If a man is making you feel like you have to compete, please dismiss him. I'm not the relationship guru, but one thing that I do know is that relationships tend to go south when someone feels threatened by an outside party.

As a matter of fact, I'm so over competing with other women that when a dating prospect allowed that to almost be the case, I was ready to dismiss him real quick. This guy apparently didn't know how to sever ties with his ex, and when she learned about my presence in his life, she turned into "Petty Labelle." This woman would go out of her way to like and share things he posted on social media, and even tried to do things to purposely monopolize his attention. She seemed so thirsty that I was tempted to offer her a bottle of water! In any case, I was tempted to go toe to toe with her, but then I had to remember who I was and who he said I was to him. That meant that she was not my responsibility, she was his. He needed to deal with her, not me. I knew that if my presence in his life meant as much as he said it did, he would make sure that no one would threaten that space. I even began to feel sorry for her; I knew that she was worth more than what she presented.

> "I had to remember **who I was** and **who he said I was** to him."

I knew that she didn't need to chase anyone. Let me also say this: I'm not stupid: I realize that no woman is going to go that hard after a man unless she thinks she has a chance! I don't know what conversations took place in my absence regarding the two of them, and now it's irrelevant.

I'm So Over It

Ladies, if a man is truly serious about you, he will never put you in a position to feel threatened by another woman. He would never make you feel like you should be in combat mode when other women come around. It always puzzles me why women attack the other woman that their men have been cheating with. The issue should not be with the other woman, it should be with the cheating man! Now I don't think that it's a man's job to make you feel secure about yourself, but he should definitely make you feel secure in the position you have in his life. At this point, I definitely was secure in who I was as a woman, but the way he handled the situation with this other woman made me feel insecure about the exclusivity of our relationship. That didn't work for me. Boy, bye.

— · — · — · —

There is enough glory on the inside of each and every one of us; we don't have to be intimidated by anybody else's shine. Let's start supporting and building each other up instead of trying to figure out how we can top each other. There is no need to compete because what God has for you is for you: whether that is a man, a job, a position, or whatever else you desire. I vow to always support, encourage, and challenge my sisters to be even more fabulous than they already are—and I will also strive to be my own personal best. Let's all shine together so that we can give all of that glory to God!

Let no corrupting talk come out of your mouths, but only such as is good for building up, as fits the occasion, that it may give grace to those who hear.
(Ephesians 4:29)

Be Done with It...

1. Think of some successful women around you. How could you support their business, causes, ministries, etc.?

2. Have you ever had a confrontation with a woman about a man? How did you handle it? Do you think your actions were indicative of self-love or confidence?

3. What is unique about you? What could another woman glean from you?

chapter 11

I'm So Over

Taming My Body

isten here: the battle between flesh and spirit is real. Lord God, it is. I may have had an issue with competing with other women, but it was nothing like the competition that goes on between my spirit and my flesh! I believe that this battle intensifies the moment we make the decision to deny our flesh and live according to the Word of God. Making the decision to live an abstinent lifestyle is just the beginning of the battle. I will tell you all the day long that I have been delivered from a life of fornication and lust, but that doesn't mean that I don't have to still fight the temptation.

Truth be told: I've always liked sex. I wasn't always living a lifestyle with the decision to honor God with my body. I was reckless. I've had to learn that being delivered from something doesn't mean that God will take all temptation away and that I would live a life not worrying about that particular sin again. I had to realize that deliverance was a process that would require for me to die daily to my own will and desires. It is a daily decision to choose Christ instead of my flesh. It is a daily battle to be intentional in my decision to be abstinent and a daily fight to guard my soul against anything that would tempt me in that area. How many know that sometimes every day isn't a good day? Some of those days, I just wanted to forget it all and climb on top of a man! Shoot. Some of those days, I did. Biology ain't no punk: sometimes it's extremely difficult to put aside your instinctive animalistic desire to go ahead and get it on with somebody. Do you know what it's like for someone to appeal to every one of your senses, but you know you can't devour him? I'm talking about having cold sweats like I was being weaned from a crack addiction.

> "Some of those days I just wanted to **forget it all** and climb on top of a man!"

I'm sure that I wasn't alone in my frustration: I was tired of fighting this daily battle. I wanted a break from the temptation and, dare I say, I wanted a break to just indulge myself to my heart's content. I felt like I was a built up ball of sexual frustration, and I started to really closely examine this whole "Panty Power" movement I was starting. I was irritated that God would make my body work in this manner but not give me permission to indulge.

In the height of my sexual frustration, I was actually dating someone who was also abstinent. When my "yes" was "yes" his "no" was "no" and I appreciated him for being a man of God and having the strength to honor his commitment to purity. Not that we didn't come dangerously close. Not that we both weren't attracted to each other. We both knew how serious it was to disobey God and defile each other's body—it wasn't something that we were willing to do.

However, I found that when I dated someone who's "yes" was "yes" while my "yes" was "yes" it caused a huge problem. No one was holding anybody else accountable for our actions. No one loved the other enough to think about what having sex would ultimately do to the other. No one considered the cost that the other would

"No one **considered the cost** that the other would pay as a result of our sin."

pay as a result of our sin. We were thinking the same way that Amnon was thinking when he raped Tamar. It was completely selfish. Animalistic. Lust in its rawest form.

With each time that I gave in to my own lusts I realized something very important about me: my flesh was weak. I had gone all this time thinking that I had my flesh under control because I had not had sex with a man in so long, but I had let my defenses completely down. It was easy for me to have a sexless life when there was no man in it. When I opened myself to seriously dating someone again, I re-discovered the issue that I had with self-control and boundaries: I had none.

I met someone, ironically, when I was speaking about my experience being abstinent. He was gorgeous, intelligent, confident—he had a certain mystique that was hard to dismiss after our initial meeting. There was a certain look in his eyes that drew me in with each word that he spoke. I knew that I was in trouble. The thing is, he told me in early conversations that he struggled in the area of sexual purity and that he didn't think that he was the right guy for me. I. Did. Not. Listen. Before I knew it, we were at it like bunnies, and I spent weeks not knowing who I was becoming. I had to look in the mirror and truly remember who

I was and who I was no longer. I thank the Lord for always reminding me.

Connecting by Disconnecting

In my decision to live a lifestyle completely dedicated to purity, I learned something about myself. I didn't know how to fully connect with men without sex. I had been sexually intimate with almost every single person that I had ever loved, liked, or dated for a while. I had never experienced a pure relationship. I had to remember that I am much more than my sexuality and that I didn't need to use it in order to attract someone or to keep someone interested in me. This was hard.

Although I had been reduced to just being a sexual object to some men, it was hard not to view men as sexual objects, too! I think that being so sexually saturated caused me to place my sexual attraction far above other things that I should have considered when dating someone. And this is after I'd already been delivered, y'all! This is after two years of abstinence! I would literally meet a guy and then immediately envision what it would be like to have sex with him. I didn't always plan to act on it, but I was definitely curious about what some of them had going on down there.

As I continue to submit my will to God's, I've asked Him to reveal different ways that I could enjoy a man's presence without ending up tackling him by the end of the night.

1. Boundaries, Baby, Boundaries

When I used to hear the word "boundaries," I would immediately conjure up an image of me trying to cross an electric fence and getting zapped to kingdom come. My mind became littered with all types of caution signs, sirens, and any other alarms that indicated that I was moving into territory that I needed to shy away from. "Boundaries" had simply become a list of do's and don'ts.

I'm So Over It

In all actuality, boundaries could be all of those things. But in my limited thinking, I always viewed boundaries as something preventing me from proceeding to an area where I actually *wanted* to go. I had to change that. Boundaries are actually something that protects us and the relationships that that we aspire to have! Think about it this way. When we establish our own boundaries, it's like having a traveling defensive line that is ready and willing to tackle anything that is trying to attack our emotions, our spirit, and other things that we value.

So, I had to readjust the things that I allowed when entering into a romantic relationship with someone. I moved beyond "we *can't* do this or that" to "I *won't* do this or that." And here's the most mind-blowing thing I learned about myself as it pertained to establishing boundaries: I needed to shut up about it!

Do you know how many times I've told someone what I wasn't going to do or what I couldn't do? And do you also know how many times my words came to slap me because I actually did what I said I couldn't or wouldn't do? The first person who has to buy into the boundaries that you establish is you! I didn't even realize that when I told these guys about my boundaries, I was doing so because I was hoping that they would *help* me uphold them! I didn't trust myself fully to stand independently on my own boundaries! Subconsciously I was saying, "I'm telling you that I don't have overnight male company because if you ask, I might say yes. Please don't ask me; I'm not strong enough to say no." Your boundaries have to first be established within yourself, otherwise your list of "Do Not's" won't be very effective.

> "Please, don't ask me; I'm **not strong enough** to say no."

2. *Explore Non-Sexual Pleasure*

Now my creativity had to come into play. It was easy to make someone feel good with my body, but how could I get a positive reaction from a man that had nothing to do with sex? That's when I had to really tap into who I was and what made me great. Then I'd have to really take my time to get to know someone so that I could understand the type of things that he enjoyed and what brought him non-sexual pleasure. I dated one guy who felt love most when he was been supported and when someone actively supported his vision. I now had a way to communicate how I felt about him in a non-sexual way, and it brought him pleasure to see me sowing my time and energy into his projects. It brought me pleasure knowing that he appreciated that.

Another thing that I started doing was sharpening my cooking skills. I had to remember that I actually enjoyed cooking for people, and it was a way for me to really put my love into edible form. Now, in my opinion, cooking for a man is a very special treat. I'm still learning how to balance going into wifey mode and just treating someone I care about to something special. I like shopping for special ingredients that I know will make one of my dishes come alive. I enjoy the delicate and precise procedures that would ensure that the dish was mouth-watering. I am enthroned by the look on someone's face when he would come in and smell the aroma of all of the fancy dishes I had cooking. I enjoy him cleaning his plate and asking for more. That is worth more than me defiling my body and giving him an orgasm instead.

Then I had to focus on what gave *me* pleasure in a non-sexual way. This was a hard one for me to focus on, because I felt like I didn't know how to ask for what I wanted in a relationship. For so long I had a accepted a man's sex as the only way that he could provide pleasure, so when I wasn't "pleased" I immediately thought that the only way that I could be pleased was with sex. Some men weren't willing to expend the effort to find more creative ways to please me, so even they thought that their penises were the solution to every ailment. As I'm spending more time learning how to be single, I am discovering more about myself and what I like. I have no problem making those suggestions now! Ha!

3. Captivate from Within

In my studies of relationships, dating, and all that jazz, I revisited the story of Esther. I've read it countless times, but in my most recent study, I came to a startling revelation: I am convinced that King Ahasuerus had sex with Esther before she became the queen! In fact, he had sex with all of the virgins who became a part of his harem!

In the evening she would go in, and in the morning she would return to the second harem in custody of Shaashgaz, the king's eunuch, who was in charge of the concubines. She would not go in to the king again, unless the king delighted in her and she was summoned by name.

(Esther 2:14)

Here's how I came to that conclusion: when the king first summoned the women, they came to him in the evening. In present day, we know that things get poppin' in the evening! Hello, somebody! Then it says that in the *morning* she would return to the harem where the *concubines* were. Number one: the women stayed overnight. I don't think that this pagan king was just "interviewing" these women until the wee hours of the morning—as a matter of fact, I don't know too many *Christians* who can handle an overnight stay with a romantic potential. Clearly this man was using his authority and power to have sex with these women.

Number two: after the women left the king's chambers, they

didn't go back to the place where all of the virgins were held, they were sent to the place where the concubines were. In case you aren't familiar with the role of a concubine, their main purpose was to be available to the kings or rulers for sexual purposes. In the Bible, we see countless examples of a barren wife suggesting that her husband lay with one of his concubines to bear children on her behalf (Genesis 16:3; Genesis 30: 3-6). So, if the women who were spending the night with King Ahasuerus were still sexually pure, why would they have a new dwelling among women who were not?

Based on this, I'm convinced that the King slept with Esther, too. But I don't think that the king was just looking for sex, or he could have chosen a queen from among the many women he already had. Even if he didn't actually have sex with Esther, one thing is for sure: whatever he experienced with her was different from every other woman he had already met.

> [T]he king loved Esther more than all the women, and she won grace and favor in his sight more than all the virgins, so that he set the royal crown on her head and made her queen instead of Vashti.
>
> (Esther 2:17)

Inquiring minds want to know what was it about Esther that was different, exactly? I know for sure that favor followed her wherever she went! I also know that she served God! I am not saying use your churchiness to captivate a man. Shame on you if you thought that's what I meant. Know this: we have a certain type of swag and light on the inside of us that comes as a result of truly knowing God. Be that authentic person that God is still developing.

"Lead with your **presence**, not your panties!"

118

Lead with your presence, not your panties! What does it feel like to simply be around you? What do you pour into those in your life? Project your heart, your intellect, your passion, and everything else that is the core of who you are in Christ. This is an art that many of us must learn.

What You Really Need

As I battled against my body, I searched myself to really try to analyze what I actually needed that I sought in sex. I realized that more than anything I craved the intimacy, the vulnerability between myself and my partner, the sense of security, the feeling of oneness, the desire to please the person who I loved—even if it was all an illusion. What I had to realize is that most of the time, it *was* an illusion. How can I feel vulnerable and secure with someone who I don't even trust when my clothes were on? How can I feel oneness with someone who wasn't sure if we were going to even be *together*? How can I have this overwhelming desire to please someone sexually when I am displeasing God in the mist!

As frustrating as my fight with lust has been, what's keeping me is the fact that my thinking has completely changed about sex. Sure, I enjoy the physical act, but it always cost me more than I was willing to pay. When I was having sex, I could feel my life draining from me. I could feel me slipping further away from God, not because He went anywhere, but because I disconnected myself from Him. That is dangerous territory. I don't care how hot and bothered I get, nothing and nobody is worth me being outside of the will of God. Jesus is my lifeline, and the only way that I can survive is if He and His word are pumping through my veins. I cannot afford to lose in this area again.

— · — · — · —

So, if you share this frustration of celibacy, you have to change your thinking about it. God is not withholding sex because He's this big, mean, dictator and He wants us to suffer. No, not at all. He wants to protect us from everything that comes with sex outside of His plan. Remember: sex is supposed to be enjoyed within the confounds of marriage. We're the ones who perverted it and reduced it to a physical pastime. He wants to save us from the heartache of the soul-ties that we develop with men who aren't our husband. He wants us to remain whole and not scattered among the different partners who we've shared ourselves with. God wants us to be able to be completely one with the man that we marry, not struggle with intimacy because we have all of these other "ones" still dwelling among us.

No temptation has overtaken you that is not common to man. God is faithful, and he will not let you be tempted beyond your ability, but with the temptation he will also provide the way of escape, that you may be able to endure it.

(1 Corinthians 10:13)

Video Bonus: "Are You a Thirsty After-thot?"

Be Done with It...

1. Do you struggle to remain abstinent in relationships because you feel that you don't know how to express love beyond the physical? What could you do experience intimacy without sexual activity?

2. What boundaries do you think are necessary for you to construct so that you are reminded not to compromise your sexual integrity?

chapter 12

I'm So Over

The Perfect Man

We've all got our "list", right? You know the list: he's got to be "this" tall, and make "this" amount of money, and drive "this" type of car—he's got to be sensitive yet strong, muscular with "good hair," smart, multi-talented, a social phenomenon, true to his inner "thug" but cries during romantic movies, no baby mamas, no past mistakes—and non-existent. One of my favorite comedians, Kev-On-Stage, made a video in which he jokes about how single women's standards change dramatically the longer we're single. He's not wrong.

But I had an inward beef with God about that. Why couldn't I just "decree and declare" the type of man that I wanted to be with and the Lord just poof him into my life? I guess I figured out that it just didn't work like that (squinting my eyes). Of course,

I had to have standards, but I had to figure out what the foundation of those standards were and where everything else fell in place. I had to adjust what I wanted in a man so that I could actually identify things that I needed to be more flexible with. It's true: the longer I remained single, the longer I did have to consider if the things I thought were "must haves" were actually things I *had* to have. I had to come to grips with the fact that my "ideal" mate simply did not exist, but the right mate does. I am no longer in pursuit of the perfect guy, but I did have to determine those qualities that I absolutely could not budge on. In lieu of my newfound "wokeness, I scaled my list down to six attributes (that's right only six!) that are a must when I'm seriously considering a man romantically.

1. He has to be a man of God.

This is something that I learned that I could not, under any circumstances, compromise. And I admit, I've met some incredible guys who did not love the Lord. They didn't understand why it couldn't work out between us, but I knew why. Unequally yoked, bruh. I've heard II Corinthians 6:14 millions of times in church. I knew that you shouldn't date anybody who didn't believe in God, but I didn't understand why until much later in life (in fact, I'm still learning the implications of being unequally yoked). I also learned that it wasn't just about dating an unbeliever; the scripture could also be applied to people who are at a different level in their spiritual walk. I'm sure I'm not the only Christian woman who has dated a man who wasn't really "in to" God or was struggling with his walk. For the majority of us, those relationships never work out. Now, I do know a very select few who ended up marrying someone who was not a devout Christian and that spouse ending up growing in his or her faith. Those were, however, very isolated incidents, and usually they were already married before one spouse became a Christian. One of my good friends broke it down to me this way: the person who does not love the Lord has a stronger conviction to sin. His conviction to sin is stronger than your conviction to do right. When it becomes a battle between the two behaviors, the stronger person will influence the weaker one. Sister "Saved-and-Sanctified" might have had the purest of intentions to bring bae to Jesus, but bae ends up pulling her into sin because sin has a greater influence on him than righteousness has on her.

"Sin has a **greater influence** on him than righteousness has on her."

The only way that I can submit to my husband is if he is first submitted to God. He cannot effectively cover me, my daughter, or any future children that we may have if he does not have a relationship with God. He has to be able to be both empowered and convicted by the word of God. I am a firm believer that a man who loves God is better able to love his wife. I need that 1 Corinthians 13 type of love; I can't trust that someone who does not know God can effectively love me. In fact, when Eve was first presented to Adam, she found him already in God's presence. He wasn't relying on her to guide him in his spiritual walk, he already had a relationship with God before she even showed up. I need that man to be the spiritual authority in our household. I want my spirit to get excited when he leads me because I recognize God's voice when he speaks! Yes God!

2. He must have vision.

I cannot stress enough how important it is to have a man with a clear idea of what my future with him will entail. For me, this is the biggest compatibility item next to having a relationship with God. Actually, this is one of the reasons why it is important to have a relationship with God because the Holy Spirit will guide us

Churchboys vs. Men of God

- *Church Boys* find their identity in their affiliations, *Men of God* find their identity in Christ.

- A *Church Boy* knows the culture of church but not necessarily the heart of God.

- *Church boys* display holiness when in the eyes of the public, *Men of God* embody holiness even when no one is looking.

- *Church Boys* view church as a networking opportunity, *Men of God* view church as a worship opportunity.

- *Church Boys* serve to be seen, *Men of God* serve because there is a need.

in discovering God's will for our lives. I believe that every person should have a vision for his or her life. Who we link with should be compatible with our vision and we should be compatible with his. Proverbs 29:18 says that without a vision the people perish: without a clear direction for our relationship or our marriage, we will eventually fail.

"Every person should have a **vision** for his or her life."

You know why the children of Israel were so happy to follow Moses out of Egypt? Because he knew where they were headed. He had clear directions and a plan for how they would get to their destination. Now, we know that it took them forty years to get to the Promised Land, but there were a lot of distractions and deviations from the plan. Moses and the crew temporarily lost sight of the vision.

I don't think that a man should even entertain a woman for marriage unless he knows where he is headed. If a woman asks him where he sees himself five, ten, twenty, or even fifty years from now and he's unable to answer that, it is a red flag. Women are helpmates; how can we know how to assist a man if he doesn't even know what he needs help with!

I want a man who knows who he is and what he is called to do. Even at the age of twelve, Jesus knew his assignment and was diligent in progressing and learning how to operate in his calling!

I'm a firm believer that people should be whole before they attempt to connect their lives with someone else. I think that best thing about being single is that we have time to really get into the presence of God and learn who we are and what we are created to do. Now this doesn't even have to be deep and spiritual, I'd want to know his passions and skills and how he plans on expanding them in the future. Cool, he currently works in construction; does he see himself doing that in the long run or is there something else he's building on simultaneously? Maybe he's always wanted to open a restaurant. I'd want to know plan he has in place in order to do that? As he's giving answers to these questions, I can already see how and if I fit into that vision. Maybe he doesn't have all of the nails and bolts of it intact, but it is important that I connect myself with someone who knows where he wants to go.

What I have also learned is that sometimes we don't always know when God will take us on a new path! I certainly didn't know that I would start a business and become an author! I admire a man who is consistently seeking God about the future and willing to go where God is leading Him.

3. He has to be physically attractive

I'll catch some flak for this, but I don't care. I *must* be physically attracted to the man I'm going to spend the rest of my life with! Point blank, period. No apologies. I want to have the urge to bite my lip when I see him walk through the door! Now, as I've grown, I've learned to abandon the "prototype" that I had for the type of guys I considered to be attractive. For the longest, I had this infatuation with men with dreadlocks. My friends and I would drool over pictures with men draping their locs across their muscular oily chests. I was so sure that my husband would be a chocolate man with long beautiful locs! Then it was all about the light skin ones with light eyes. If you didn't look like Common or El Debarge, you couldn't say anything to me! Ha!

I also had to abandon the expectation that my husband had to be "movie-star" fine. I was expecting to walk down the altar and join hands with a Brian White or Chris Hemsworth look alike for sure! Now, I'm not saying that I wouldn't want to look at a gorgeous man, I'm saying that I've expanded my appreciation of multiple forms of "art," if you will. To be more specific, I used to only want a man who was muscular, but then I realized that it wasn't a realistic expectation unless I was also in shape. It then took for me to become interested in a guy who was a lot softer and more "fluffy" to realize that I actually didn't have to have a man who looks like he drinks protein shakes out of a milk jug. My attraction has expanded significantly over the years, and I've even surprised myself when thinking about some of the men I was attracted to. I no longer have a "type" when it comes to physical attributes, but I do know this: if I have to work hard to find out if I think he's cute, then it's not going to work.

Even though being physically attractive is a must-have in my future husband, we have to be careful not to be so consumed by a man's physical appearance that we ignore what's in his heart.

But the LORD said to Samuel, "Do not look on his appearance or on the height of his stature, because I have rejected him. For the LORD sees not as man sees: man looks on the outward appearance, but the LORD looks on the heart."
(I Samuel 16:7)

I've had my heart broken by the most gorgeous men in life, so good looks definitely shouldn't be the end-all-be-all. I just pray that the man I marry has a heart that is even more beautiful as his outward appearance—but Father, I'd still like for him to be fine in Jesus name, amen.

4. He has to be financially stable.

I've paid my dues as the "struggle bus" chick; I've been with men when they didn't even have a penny for my thoughts. I've lent my car, given rides to work, given money for bus fare, opened my home when lights got cut off—I've done it all. And I don't want to do it again. I feel that if a man is seriously considering marriage, he needs to be in a position to contribute to the financial well-being of his family. I'm not saying that he has to be making a six figure income and wiping his behind with dollar bills, but he needs to be making conscious moves to build a secure financial foundation. I'm not even saying that he has to be the sole bread-winner for our family: I'm okay with him bringing home the bacon and me bringing home the eggs. It would be nice if he could handle all of our expenses with his income, but I'm perfectly okay with having a great financial co-dependency with my husband.

The Bible even says that before you consider making a major decision you should count the cost of it.

For which of you, desiring to build a tower, does not first sit down and count the cost, whether he has enough to complete it? Otherwise, when he has laid a foundation and is not able to finish, all who see it begin to mock him, saying, 'This man began to build and was not able to finish.'"
(Luke 14:28-30)

I often scratch my head at men who date women when they don't have their finances together or at least have a plan to be financially stable. Is it the expectation that every woman will be that "ride or die" chick and stay with this man until he's able to get it together? Imagine what it would be like as a man to not consider the financial responsibility of marriage and be unable to make provisions for your family? What woman would marry a man and anticipate being in poverty?

I can't wait for the conversation when I get to ask, "So how do you go about budgeting your money? Do you have a savings account? How is your retirement plan set up? Do you have any debt, if so, are you consciously making timely payments so that your debt does not negatively affect your credit? Do you tithe? Are you a giver?"

Some might think that this is ridiculous, but every married couple I know has told me that you need to ask these types of questions before you consider marrying someone. Especially because many marriages end in divorce due to some type of financial strain! Not I. Because I want a man who is a good steward over his finances, I'm diligently working on cleaning up mine. When he asks me those questions, I want to be able to also answer in full confidence.

Now the reality is that financial issues may present themselves at some point in a relationship and marriage. I definitely wouldn't just up and leave a man who was experiencing such hardship. In fact, if we were married that means I've already vowed to be with him for richer and for poorer anyway! I think that there is a stark difference between a man who is not wise with his finances and one who happens to be experiencing some financial hardship. In any case, finances are extremely important to me, so I gotta have a man who also shares the same type of financial reverence.

> "There is stark **difference** between a man who is not wise with his finances and one experiencing hardship."

5. He must be intelligent.

This seems like a no-brainer (no pun intended), but I've talked to so many handsome hollow shells. I've grown frustrated attempting to have conversations with men and trying to restrain myself from ripping them into shreds for being so ignorant. I'm over the whole "He has to be an Ivy League grad with an advanced degree" thing. As a matter of fact, I don't think I'd mind if he didn't have a degree at all. I know some idiots with several degrees. However, I am a life-long learner, so I'd like to be married to someone who is open to learning new things and can share those new perspectives with me. Challenge my mind. Hush me with your knowledge! Ha!

"**Challenge me** with your mind. **Hush me** with your knowledge!"

Even if he isn't the most educated man, I absolutely will not go for a fool. As a matter of fact, I'm well within my biblical rights to want an intelligent man. The Bible tells me to remove myself from the presence of a foolish man (Proverbs 14:7)! I used to hear the phrase "Common sense ain't common anymore." I don't want to be led by someone who makes foolish mistakes because he rejects knowledge and wisdom.

My heart actually goes out to my girl Abigail in the Bible; she married an incredibly foolish man by the name of Nabal. David and his men had been very kind to Nabal's servants, and in exchange, David asked if Nabal could give them provisions for their journey. Instead of doing the honorable and sensible thing and giving David what he had asked for, Nabal rejected the request. Because of Nabal's blatant disrespect, David was ready to come and attack with all four hundred of his men!

Now what's interesting to me in this story is that one of Nabal's servants reached out to Nabal's wife and asked for her help.

---

*Now therefore know this and consider what you should do,
for harm is determined against our master and against all
his house, and he is such a worthless man that one cannot
speak to him.*

(1 Samuel 25:17)

Nabal's issue wasn't just that he was a fool. No, no. His issue was that he was a fool who couldn't be told anything. He rejected and wasn't even open to hearing sound counsel. That's the worst kind! His foolishness was actually going to bring harm to everyone in his household. Good thing Nabal married a shrewd woman, otherwise everyone would be left to the mercy of David and his army. I actually dated a guy who couldn't take correction and rebuke from anyone, and he was always "right" about everything. I learned quickly that the days of our relationship were truly numbered. I have to have a man with some sense! For the sake of my household!

I think that it takes a very mature person to recognize that he doesn't know it all or have all the answers. I think it takes an even more mature person to seek the knowledge and wisdom they don't have. James 1:5 even tells us that if we lack wisdom, we should ask God. Why we a fool when we have access to a God who gives wisdom liberally!

6. He must have integrity.

I think moral uprightness is more attractive on a man than any of his other attributes. Even more than his beard. I love beards, so having integrity is a big deal to me. Ha! For example: one of my biggest pet peeves when it comes to relationships in general is having to deal with a person who does not keep his word.

I mean, it bothers me to my absolute core, partly because I grew up having that be a consistent reality. It's a terrible feeling to look forward to something time and time again only to have people let you down and show no remorse for it. It's an even more terrible thing to no longer believe people when they say that they will do something because you conditioned not to honor their words.

I want to be able to trust my man. I want his words to be worth more than the money in his bank account. I want to know without a shadow of a doubt that who he is in public is also who he is privately. A man who can do the right thing simply because it is the right thing is a man who'd have my heart for sure.

I want my man to have that Joseph level integrity. First and foremost, Joseph was fine (Genesis 39:6). See, even the Bible justifies me wanting to marry a fine man! Joseph had been working in Potiphar's house as a servant, and then Potiphar's wife started to notice just how fine Joseph was. She tried to seduce him on several occasions, but Joseph was so integrous that he denied her every time. Think about it: he probably could have had whatever he wanted if he agreed to this arrangement with Potiphar's wife. He probably would have been able to get away with it because this adulterous wife surely wouldn't tell her husband. He could have bowed before Potiphar by day and had Potiphar's wife bowing before him by night. When he denied her for the last time, she falsely accused Joseph of trying to rape her—she was offended that his honor meant more to him than her body.

Joseph had declared that he was a man of God, so he was determined to let his actions support his declaration. I don't expect to marry a blind man, so I know that he'll come across other beautiful women from time to time. I also know that there will be other women who will be attracted to him. I want to be with a man who I know will make the right decision even when he is faced with temptation.

What I also noticed about Joseph is that because he was a man of integrity, God's favor always followed him. When Joseph was working in Potiphar's house, God caused that house to be prosperous. Even when Joseph was in prison, his integrity caused him to be elevated and placed in charge of all of the other prisoners. And let's not even talk about when he was in the palace with pharaoh. He was honored and placed in a position that caused him to be able to bless his family. I want the blessings of God to be upon my household because my husband is a man of integrity. Because he's following Christ not just in word but in deed. I'm also excited that his integrity will be modeled for our children to witness and emulate in the future.

— · — · — · —

I've decided to put aside my impossible list of "must-haves" to really determine the qualities that are the most important when choosing a husband. Yes, having a millionaire husband would be nice, but what if I still feel lonely with him? Or having a husband who looks like walking perfection would be great, but what good is looking at a gorgeous man who I do not trust? I'm so over choosing men based on temporary or shallow attributes.

[M}ake every effort to supplement your faith with virtue, and virtue with knowledge, and knowledge with self-control, and self-control with steadfastness, and steadfastness with godliness, and godliness with brotherly affection, and brotherly affection with love.

(2 Peter 1:5-7)

Be Done with It...

1. What qualities do you desire in a mate?

2. Based on that list, what things are negotiable and what things are non-negotiable?

3. Is there a possibility that you may have overlooked a great guy because of some unrealistic expectation on your list?

chapter 13

I'm So Over

God's Jealousy

*I*t's ridiculous, I know. Some have no idea of what it truly means for God to be "jealous for us." If you're like me, you fell in love with the song "How He Loves Us" which talks about just how much God loves us. I'll give you the link to the song so we're on the same page.

There is no question, this song has to positively affect the heart of anyone who has a personal relationship with God. It has so much imagery and overall "feel goodness:" it makes your heart just flutter thinking about God. But I think that a lot of people ignore the first line of that song, or they either don't really understand the implications for God being "jealous for" them.

I think I know, and I had an attitude about it.

So watch yourselves, that you do not forget the covenant of the LORD your God which He made with you, and make for yourselves a graven image in the form of anything against which the LORD your God has commanded you. For the LORD your God is a consuming fire, a jealous God.

(Deuteronomy 4:23-24)

So let me tell you about this terrible habit that I know God wasn't happy about. Usually, when I wasn't dating or entertaining anyone, I was gung-ho for Jesus. I mean, praying for people, going to Bible studies, reading Christian literature, singing, ministering in some shape, form or fashion. Then it seemed like every time I thought I was in a "good place" in my walk with God, I caught the eye of some dashingly handsome man, and all of that giddiness and availability that I was giving God was going straight to him. I mean, fine men, too. Lord, help me.

Now, in my opinion, I didn't completely lose myself to the point of thoroughly forsaking God. I didn't become a Muslim just because brotha Kareem had a nice beard and pretty eyes. I wasn't cussing or drinking if I had happened upon a man who was participating in those actions. I still loved Jesus and was still "pressing towards the mark". But when someone was able to really get my attention, it became far too easy to give my time and affection to these guys. I was giving God scraps from the time that I had left over. I would notice my prayer life becoming more and more stale, and that I had been giving in to different compromises here and there. I was consumed with thoughts of whatever man I was interested in. In the relationships that I wrote about in my first book, The Power of the Panties, those compromises were deadly and extreme. I'm grateful that God would not allow me to continue in those relationships, and I'm so glad that He protected me.

Here's where my irritation came into play: I felt like God was blocking a little too much. Even when I was meeting Christian men, I could still feel the Holy Spirit telling me to fall back a little. I would lament that this was a man of God, what could be wrong! I was annoyed to say the least. It's almost like I knew exactly when my convictions would "flare up," and I had to end the relationship. I would also know when the guy was going to give me my exit ticket and break up with me. It had become routine, and I was just too through with God. I thought that it was too hard to try to maintain a relationship with a man and try to maintain the one that I have with Him, too. I had no idea why God would shut down relationships with perfectly good godly men.

Well, except that most of them weren't perfectly good godly men at all. I wasn't exactly all the way godly myself. Here's the thing: we are in covenant with God. There is no other person on this earth that I have that type of relationship with. We have a blood-bond: there was literally blood shed for God to procure the right to call me His own. When I accepted Jesus Christ as my Lord and Savior, I made a life-long agreement to surrender my will to God's. It is a bond that I made with Him for all of eternity. It's stronger than the bond that I have with my parents and siblings. More absolute than the one that I'll have with my husband. I was bought with a price, and how great that price was!

I Left My First Love

But I have this [charge] against you, that you have left your first love [you have lost the depth of love that you first had for Me].

(Revelation 2:4, Amplified)

139

I had to reflect. How can I love someone else when I had a disconnection with "Love" Himself? How could I continuously pour out love and not spend time with God so that He could pour love into me? Christ needs to be the foundation for any relationship that we have. The Bible says

> "Instead of clinging to **God** as the foundation for any relationship, I clung to the **man.**"

that we are the branch and that Christ is the vine: a part from Him, we can do nothing (John 15:5). That includes having a loving and sustainable relationship. Think about the structure of a cross: the horizontal part is supported by the vertical part, which is anchored into the ground. The vertical part of the cross represents our relationship with God. It is the anchor and support to all of the other relationships that we have. It we have not made sure that the foundation is secure, our other relationships will be flimsy and weak. They will not be able to stand. So how could I really be upset with God about failed relationships when He wasn't even the anchor for them? Instead of clinging to God as the foundation for any relationship, I clung to the man: he one who cannot compare to my God.

The Boring Wife

I think that in my years of being in a covenant relationship with God, I grew into an old boring wife. You know the ones I'm talking about: the ones who've been cooking the same meals day in and out, the ones who have been wearing the same hairstyle for years on end, the ones who have been making love to their husbands the same way every time—the ones who have grown complacent and stagnant in their marriages. I believe that I had gotten that way with God and my complacency was why it was so important for me to be with a man. It was also why I was so irritated when things didn't work out with that man. I had to come to the realization that my relationship with God was extremely— blah.

I'm on a journey, and I need to rekindle who God is to me. He's still that "hunk" that I fell in love with when I was a fifteen-year-old girl reading Bible stories in the wee hours of the morning. He's still that same God whose presence I could feel whenever I would open up my mouth to worship Him. The same God who would wipe my tears and give me constant reminders of how much I meant to Him and how I was always on His mind. He still has the flame that can set my heart on fire, but I boxed Him out because of how familiar He had become to me. How did I reduce my relationship with Him to a couple of metaphorical dry pecks on the cheek? How dare I come before

> "I boxed him out because of how **familiar He had become** to me."

Him asking about a husband when I was such a mediocre wife to Him? He has every right to be jealous because I longed to give my heart away to someone when He didn't fully have it anymore. The nerve.

Are You Thirsty?

I always love the stories in the Bible where Jesus directly interacts with women. I can always see myself in those pages, and I always receive a great revelation from the conversations that he has with them. Let's talk a little bit about the Samaritan woman found in the fourth chapter of John.

Jesus had just finished healing and ministering to some people when He and his disciples decided to travel through Samaria. Jesus decided to stop by the infamous "Jacob's Well" because he was thirsty. In his quest for water, he was met by a woman from Samaria. He began to chat with her a little. She found it rare that Jesus, a Jew, would even converse with her considering that she was a Samaritan.

The conversation between the two continued, and Jesus got all in her business rather quickly. He reminded her how she had five husbands and how the one she was with currently wasn't even her husband! Oop! Had that been me, I would have been ready to fight! Ha! But Jesus didn't just tell her that information about herself to shame her, He did it because He needed her to know the extent of His identity. This wasn't just an ordinary Jew she was shooting the breeze with: she had been face to face with her King and Redeemer. She was exchanging words with the Lover of her soul.

Jesus revealing the Samaritan woman's past wasn't his main reason for talking to her. What He imparted to her was far more important:

[W]hoever drinks of the water that I will give him will never be thirsty again. The water that I will give him will become in him a spring of water welling up to eternal life.''
(John 4:13-14)

I was that Samaritan woman. What I noticed about her is that she had attempted to fill a void with the presence of men. There was something that she was searching for—desperately—that she could not find within these countless relationships she entertained. What I love about having a relationship with God is that He's always sharpening and pruning us so that He can continue to get glory from our lives. While I have been delivered from sexual sin and the thought that I had to give my body to different men in order to have a sense of fulfillment, God revealed that I was still looking for fulfillment in men.

It was no accident that the Samaritan woman was at the well: she was both literally and spiritually thirsty. It was no wonder that I had entertained countless unproductive and toxic relationships: I was thirsty! Though God was patching up my heart, there was still a hole there that I had to surrender. I don't want to keep thirsting and going on an endless quest to be fulfilled by a man; I want to already be satisfied in Christ!

I love the part when He tells her that his water will well up to eternal life. His substance makes us whole. His substance revitalizes us and makes us powerful and renewed. He has every right to be jealous when we attempt to put people before Him because He knows that what we seek and thirst after can only be fulfilled through Him. He knows that He is the only one who knows us intimately enough to give us exactly what we need. He made preparations for us to spend eternal life with Him. How dare we abandon God and put Him on the back burner for mere mortal men?

So my resolve was not to be "angry" with God because I thought that he was blocking me from being with men who I so desperately wanted to be with. Instead, I am grateful that my God is protecting me from things that I cannot foretell. I am grateful that He has taken the charge of protecting my heart—even if I have to turn down some beautiful prospects in the process.

- · - · - · -

God loves us so much that He's always thinking about us. We're always on his mind. We have to remember that if nobody else is on our team, God is. If a hundred men declare their love and allegiance to us and then leave us the very next day, God is going to be the one who will always be there because of how much He loves us. When we really spend time in the presence of God, and when we spend time studying and getting to know Him, the residue of His glory is evident. We start to reflect who He is. People should be able to look at us and notice that there's something special about us. People should be able to sense God's presence even if they don't actually know that the extra sparkle or glow that we have is directly related to God.

When we're sincerely content with having a relationship with God alone, we wear that sense of wholeness and fulfillment like a jacket. As a matter of fact, when you have that special type of adornment, you'll be surprised who you will attract. I'm a firm believer that when we become our best "selves" we attract the person who is best for us. For me, I can't be my best self unless God is involved. My best self is only who God intended for me to be. So when my focus shifted to becoming my best, I can now expect God's best for me.

The Heart Sings

My soul longs and thirsts after You
Your presence quinches a parchness from Your well of life
I am patiently planted for an outpouring of Your love
You have created in me a most ferocious desire
For You, in all of Your fullness, in Your entirety
My mind replays your alluring scent
And Your embrace that makes me giddy with infatuation
My walls fall when You are near, my inhibitions cease
You gently peel away the masks that disguise my imperfections
So that I am thoroughly exposed and naked before You
Yet You cover me

I follow hard after You
Magnetically drawn to every move that You make
Denouncing myself and my own directions
To tread the path that You've paved for me

I'm So Over It

My soul sounds a siren of obsession unto you
Pacing the door of your dwelling place like a senseless fiend
Overtaken by Your words of affirmation and Your love language
That transcends the realm of intelligible comprehension
Lord, I leak with constant adoration and exaltation of You
My mouth expels whimpers of my overwhelming fire for You
Love is too incomplete to reflect my disposition
But I am limited in my vocabulary

I long to experience You in all of Your glory
To reach complete unification
To bask in the warmth of your aura
To be pollenated with your splendor and majesty
To be loosed from my physical limitations
To experience You purely and wholly

I have loved you with an everlasting love; therefore I have
continued my faithfulness to you.
(Jeremiah 31:3)

Be Done with It...

1. Have you found yourself dating multiple people or jumping from relationship to relationship in order to fill a void?

2. What could you do to improve your relationship with God? How could you show God that He is first priority in your life?

I'm Moving on from It

$\mathcal{I}$ hope that you'll be happy to know that I no longer want to become a nun. Thank God for deliverance! Ha! I am in an awesome place because I chose to give every bit of frustration that I was feeling to the Lord. Throughout this process I've gotten to know Him as something else: a best friend. Sure, the Bible tells us that He calls us friend, but I've never known what that felt like until now. I told Him things that I never wanted to tell anyone else, and He never met me with wrath. He met me with love and understanding. He wiped my tears when my heart was breaking into sand. He checked me when I would say things that were truly and utterly ridiculous. He affirmed me, and reminded me just how beautiful I am. When I wanted to go away from Him, He even let me blame Him! But He also directed me to the truth and was patient with me as I learned it. He challenged me to take responsibility for what I allowed into my life. What better friend than that?

And let me say this, too: it wasn't just Jesus who helped me deal with all of the toxicity and brokenness inside of me. I sought professional help! Yes, I was telling a complete stranger about my childhood, my patterns, my pain, my struggles, and my fears. I fought past the stigma of being labeled "crazy" because I solicited the help of a life coach. It was uncomfortable, but it was the best investment that I had ever made in myself! In meeting with my coach regularly, I was able to identify and deal with things that I never thought about before! I'd never even considered them to be issues! If I could give you any practical advice, please get some type of counseling! Even if you don't think anything is "wrong, you'll be amazed at how much opportunity there is to grow and heal!

I am free, my loves, I am! I write this with tears in my eyes because it feels so good to be able to say it! And loudly! I'm not warring against these same things anymore because I have solidified my deliverance this day! I am excited about my future because I have appropriately dealt with my past. And should these thoughts and habits try to creep up on me again, I got some'n for 'em!

It is my absolute desire to see women living out their lives in the splendor and glory that God had bestowed upon us. I want women to walk in victory and wear that victory better than the best designer bag you can find! It is my sincerest prayer that some sentence, some word, or some phrase has ignited a fire within you to truly seek wholeness in our Heavenly Father. I pray that you abandon any thoughts, habits, or people that would rob you of every good thing that you desire from the Lord. I am excited about where God is taking you, and I celebrate you for being enchanting, empowered, and impactful. May God bless you, and may He wow you with His wonders!

About the Author

Kierra C. Jones is not only an author, she is a speaker, teacher, and visionary. As author of *The Power of the Panties: Overcoming Sexual Bondage* and founder of the "Panty Power" movement, her mission is to impact women with the message of deliverance through Jesus Christ, to support women facing issues in sexual integrity, and to help women foster a healthy self-image. Kierra is active in ministry as a worship leader, songwriter, intercessor, and author. She currently resides in Detroit, MI with her daughter, Kasey.

As a youth, Kierra was always drawn to women's ministry. In college, she joined Alpha Omega Co-Ed Christian Fraternity, Inc., at Grand Valley State University. While apart of Alpha Omega, Kierra taught Bible studies that were tailormade for college-aged women. Kierra also spent time working at a youth residential program where she used her many gifts to show the love of Christ to teenage girls. She has spoken at conferences and seminars with the goal of empowering women to live a lifestyle that is pleasing to God. Kierra has also been featured on The Word Network's 910Am Superstation radio shows "Live with David Bullock", "Life in the D" with Judge Vonda Evans and Councilwoman Mary Sheffield, and the "Greg Davis Show". Her approach to ministry is that it should meet people where they are by being both spiritual and relevant.

www.ingramcontent.com/pod-product-compliance
Lightning Source LLC
Chambersburg PA
CBHW031959080426
42735CB00007B/441